5 Survivors

5 Survivors

Personal Stories of Healing from PTSD and Traumatic Events

Tracy Stecker, Ph.D.

HAZELDEN®

Hazelden
Center City, Minnesota 55012
hazelden.org

Library of Congress Cataloging-in-Publication Data

Stecker, Tracy, 1969–
    5 survivors : personal stories of healing from PTSD and traumatic events / Tracy Stecker.
       p.   cm.
    ISBN 978-1-61649-093-5 (pbk.)
    1. Post-traumatic stress disorder—Case studies. 2. Post-traumatic stress disorder—Treatment. I. Title. II. Title: Five survivors.
    RC552.P67S737 2011
    616.85'21—dc23

                                        2011019395

In the stories that follow, names have been changed to protect the privacy of the victims of trauma as well as those who know them.

The photograph on page 166 is reprinted with the permission of an anonymous photographer.

15 14 13 12 11   1 2 3 4 5 6

Cover design by Theresa Jaeger Gedig
Interior design by David Spohn
Typesetting by BookMobile Design and Publishing Services, Minneapolis, Minnesota

Contents

	INTRODUCTION	ix
CHAPTER 1	Victim of Abuse: Ren's Story	1
CHAPTER 2	Beads: Hershel's Story	53
CHAPTER 3	The Storm before the Calm: Alex's Story	85
CHAPTER 4	Disaster: Ray's Story	109
CHAPTER 5	Buddies: Joseph's Story	139
	EPILOGUE	169

Introduction

THIS BOOK REPRESENTS A LABOR OF LOVE. I remember the idea of publishing people's stories of trauma and recovery tickling me for months. I am not an author, however, so I batted the idea away as quickly as it came. Yet it kept coming back.

In my work I regularly talk to soldiers returning from the wars in Iraq and Afghanistan. Although I trained as a clinician, I primarily conduct research developing and investigating ways to increase the seeking of mental health treatment by those who would benefit from it. This means that I frequently come in contact with individuals severely in need of help who do not receive it. As a researcher, I focus on data, not stories. Yet some of the stories I heard haunted me.

My life changed the day I formally decided to record some of those stories. You might wonder how someone trained as a psychologist, in the roles of both clinician and researcher, could possibly make such a radical shift. I'll tell you how. Clinicians do not become their patients or clients. We embrace the moment in the session, but it does not change us. This is even more true for researchers. We see data and patterns, not people. In choosing to tell these stories, I embraced trauma intimately. The result was fantastically heart wrenching.

Posttraumatic stress disorder (PTSD) is an anxiety disorder that develops after exposure to an extremely traumatic stressor involving actual or threatened death or serious injury. The response to the stressor must involve intense fear, helplessness, or horror.

Characteristic symptoms resulting from the exposure include (1) re-experiencing, in the form of flashbacks or nightmares; (2) avoidance of stimuli associated with the trauma; and (3) persistent increased arousal.

A frequent consequence of PTSD is that the individual becomes intensely uncomfortable, both physically and psychologically, when exposed to triggers that remind him or her of the traumatic event. Examples of triggers may include anniversaries, weather, weapons, or stories that are similar. These triggers tend to be persistently avoided. The individuals may make a constant effort to avoid situations, thoughts, or feelings they might associate with the trauma. The avoidance may be severe enough that it resembles amnesia regarding aspects of the traumatic event. Associated with this avoidance is a "numbness" or general lack of responsiveness to other aspects of life. For example, many wives of soldiers returning from the wars in Iraq and Afghanistan report that their spouses "changed" during the war. A common description is that the couple used to have fun together but that the returning partner no longer seems to experience fun and is not interested in engaging in playful activities.

Along with this numbness is an associated hyperarousal or hyper-vigilance (always being on the alert). These same wives report that although their husbands used to be fun, now they are more concerned about weapons and locking doors at night. Marked outbursts of anger are common among individuals suffering from PTSD. Symptoms of hyperarousal or hypervigilance could include difficulty falling or staying asleep, outbursts of anger and irritability, difficulty concentrating, and exaggerated startle response.

Many individuals suffering from exposure to traumatic events do not run around talking about their trauma. I repeat this point because these five survivors were courageous enough to share their stories. The diagnostic handbook for physicians and mental health providers gives the following information about avoiding stimuli associated with trauma:

Persistent avoidance of stimuli associated with the trauma and numbing of general responsiveness as indicated by three or more of the following:

(a) efforts to avoid thoughts, feelings, or conversations associated with the trauma
(b) efforts to avoid activities, places, or people that arouse recollections of the trauma
(c) inability to recall an important aspect of the trauma
(d) markedly diminished interest or participation in significant activities
(e) feeling of detachment or estrangement from others
(f) restricted range of affect (unable to have loving feelings)
(g) sense of foreshortened future

There are a couple of things you must understand before reading these stories of survival from trauma and traumatic experiences. These survivors shared their stories with me out of a desperate need to heal and to be helpful to others who have experienced trauma or who love someone who has experienced trauma. In my position, I am all too aware of how many of you out there silently suffer from traumatic experiences, and this book is for you. The individuals in this collection told the stories of their own need to heal and help. They were not paid, and talking about their lives was not easy. You will notice that trust is not a key characteristic among individuals who have experienced trauma, yet these courageous five were brave enough to trust me to tell you their stories. And the process was painful. I am honored to have been part of this work. I loved every second talking to these people and writing their stories. For the first time in my career, I felt blessed. I knew I was being given a tremendous opportunity. It was a gift I now hand over to you. I hope you all appreciate, as I do, the effort it took for these five to share.

CHAPTER 1

Victim of Abuse: Ren's Story

BEFORE TRAUMA: **The Traveling Salesman**

REN SAYS HER EARLIEST MEMORIES involved her father. She remembers him holding her in a rocking chair to soothe away an earache. She also remembers him laughing at something she said, but it was unclear whether he was laughing at or with her. The look on her face suggests she is still confused about the incident. She sits in a chair with her arms crossed and looks out the window into the woods. Her thoughts feel far away as she talks about her childhood personality. She describes herself as watchful, quiet, the kind of child who liked to blend into the background and observe those around her. In seeing her sitting in that chair, you could almost imagine her as a little girl. She blends in without calling attention to herself. She says she was part of the world, more or less, until her father attended to her. At those moments, she was special. "But I could never quite figure out how to consistently be special. There seemed some diaphanous line between special and abhorrent that was hard to predict."

When he decided I was special, he would tell people that I was his daughter and that I was smart. Beautiful. He would wear a proud smile on his face that seemed to indicate that he meant every single word. His eyes would shine with love. My father was a traveling salesman and would be gone on trips for many weeks of the year. Whenever he returned from a trip, he would bring a present for me. I remember one time in particular he came home after spending two weeks in Paris. He brought me a music box. It was about the size of my hand, and when you opened the lid, you could see the wheel turning for the music to play. There was a little section that would hold something small. Maybe a ring or a necklace. Perhaps a coin. The picture on the top of the music box was a puppy. A little beagle puppy. I remember cherishing that music box. When I would open it and listen to the music and see the red felt inside and the wheel turning, I believed in magic and love. Touching that music box allowed me to touch the feeling of love. Someone in the world loved me, and this box was an actual concrete expression of that love.

My mother did not receive gifts from my father and held these treasures in great contempt. My father would sometimes bring home gifts that were impractical. My brother, for example, would get a shirt typically worn in India. This was not a shirt he could get away with actually wearing in our small town. A ten-year-old boy couldn't wear that type of shirt without looking funny. It seemed in my town that people did what you expected them to do. So boys wore T-shirts and jeans and sneakers. I can't even remember anyone who did otherwise, although I suppose it's possible. I know my brother wasn't the type to choose otherwise. My father seemed hardly aware of these practicalities. He wanted us to see the magic. Like the magic I saw in the music box. If only that same magic could be seen in that shirt. It was probably easier for me because I really wanted to believe.

While my father was a romantic, he also had a terrible temper. He was a violent man. My youngest brother got the worst of it. It seemed to me that he could and would kill my brother one day. His anger was out of control.

An example of my father's rage happened one time when my brothers and I were running around the house playing some type of game of chase or something. I knocked over an aquarium that was sitting in the formal living room. Our house was a two-story house with a basement. The lower level had a family room, kitchen, formal living room, and a dining room. In the middle was a staircase going upstairs, so it was perfect for children to run around in a circle. The aquarium I knocked over was small. It was about twelve inches high and held small rocks, a fake plant, and a tiny frog. As far as I know, there was nothing particularly special about this aquarium. Maybe [it was] some kind of decoration, although it never occurred to me to ask who brought it home or who picked it out. It's conceivable the aquarium had some special meaning and I just didn't know about it.

My father got home from work that day and just about killed my younger brother. I remember hearing the sounds of a beating and my father screaming. Guttural sounds. Immense terror filled my heart. I ran as fast as I could to my brother's room upstairs, where the sounds were. In the room, my brother was lying on his back on his bed with his arms up, trying to protect himself from the punches. His face contorted with fear and he looked red all over. Mostly I saw cowering and terror. He was only seven or eight years old. Standing over him was my father, who was swinging with what appeared to be all his strength. He punched and punched, and from my point of view, he was deliberate with the punches only in the purpose of connecting. He wanted to hurt him.

I howled and jumped onto my father's back. I wrapped my arms around his arms so that he could no longer swing so easily. I was not looking anywhere but focusing my whole being on preventing those arms from swinging again. I closed my eyes to garner every bit of strength inside me.

To my surprise, my father stopped swinging. His arms fell, his head dropped, and he stopped. I slid off him because he had stopped. He turned away from me and walked out of the room.

Odd how the scene changed. One moment my brother and I had our eyes focused on my father and his wild swinging, and a second later my father had left the room and I was looking at my brother. [It was as if] a tornado had swept through the room. There one moment, gone the next.

My brother was still lying on the bed. Sobbing. Fear and terror slowly evaporating into a scene of grief and shame. Our heads faced downward, and we were unwilling to meet each other's eyes.

I, too, left the room. I had to find my father. While his rage was ending, mine was building.

I headed down the hallway to pursue him. I felt a determination to make things right. I would find him and convince him he was not allowed to treat children like that. It wasn't normal. It wasn't right. It wasn't healthy and it wasn't good. There was nothing good about it and it had to stop.

I found him in my room. He was sitting on my bed, sobbing, holding his face in his hands. He looked up when I walked in and asked me to sit with him. I was obedient even when enraged, so I sat.

We sat quietly for a moment or two and he cried. While he cried, I saw shame and embarrassment. Shame oozed out of his tears. I couldn't bear to see my father so ashamed. It was excruciating to watch a parent lose control over a situation and even worse to watch his awareness of his inadequacy. In my head, watching my father's shame was as bad as watching the beating.

A beating is a physical event with a beginning and an end. A victim and a perpetrator. Shame is an emotional event with no boundaries. It feels limitless and, to my young mind, crushes the core of the person. The soul cannot be free when there is shame.

I wanted to believe my father felt remorse. His tears confirmed for me what I believed. He behaved atrociously and he knew it. Since he got it, it would stop and this would never happen again. So I believed it was now my job to build him back up.

He said, "Baby, I am a bad father. I want you and your brothers to have all the things I didn't have when I was a child. I work hard to provide for you. I don't want you to see me like this."

He was sitting on my bed and I couldn't bear his disappointment. I wanted to believe that he understood what he had done. So I said, "Dad, it's OK. You do provide for us. You work hard and give us everything we need. You are a good father."

I put my hand on his shoulder and turned to look in his eyes so he knew that I meant it.

He said, "No, I am a terrible father and I've let you down."

I had to convince him. "You are a good father. You would do anything to make sure we have everything we need."

I rationalized. He had been through so much in his life that it only made sense that he acted the way he did. It was what he knew. Through my forgiveness and acceptance of him, he would be able to see himself in a different way and no longer have to behave with such rage and anger and violence. My forgiveness would be healing.

It turned out that my father would only apologize to me for his violence. He never apologized to my brother.

I've carried a lot of guilt about that. I wasn't even the one who got hit. That time.

It turned out the entire incident was due to his coming home and seeing the aquarium in pieces on the living room floor. Something I had knocked over. This was only one incident in a world of many. Violence was a definite part of our lives.

I grew up in a violent home. The worst part for me at the time was watching my brothers get hurt. In hindsight, the part that hurt me the worst was the shame. And the fear of losing my father's love. One time, he took our family out to dinner. We drove about half an hour away from our town to go somewhere "special." A steakhouse! Steakhouses were meaningless to me, but they held enormous value to my father. I couldn't seem to understand how the steakhouse made us special, but it was clear that on those nights, my father would puff up with pride. Boy, was he proud of himself and his accomplishments. We were expected to dress up and to put on our best manners. For me, this meant I was expected to wear a dress and keep absolutely quiet. I was there for appearances, not for personality. Unfortunately, my brother made me giggle during dinner. He accidentally made a funny noise with an ice cube at the table, and the noise shocked him. He must've also understood that he was there for appearances and not personality. His shock at his own noise amused me, and I laughed. The repercussion for that laugh was a dirty look from my father, who suddenly had an incredible amount of tension in his mouth (as though he were doing his very best to hold back his rage). The tension in my father's face remained throughout the rest of the dinner, and I was told that I was no longer his daughter for making a scene out at a restaurant. I was disowned on the car ride back home.

It wasn't the only time I was disowned, but it may have been the only time I was disowned for giggling.

Checkup

When I was eight years old, I went to my annual physical. I remember my mother taking me to the appointment. My doctor had been our family physician my whole life, although I don't remember us ever visiting the doctor unless it was for our annual physical. We didn't have many health problems in our family, except I remember once that my youngest brother broke his arm falling out of a tree in our backyard, and my middle brother had appendicitis. As far as I know, we were physically healthy otherwise.

For this checkup, my mother and I were in the waiting room until we were called. It never took very long for us to be called back into the room. The receptionist told us it was our time to go back and we were shown the room. In those days, the rooms were actually two rooms. To get to the exam room, you had to walk through another room, which contained chairs and a table. I suppose this was an area where family members could wait in private while the doctor examined the patient. Funny how we don't have that setup anymore. Actually, I have no idea if that was a typical setup or if it was unique to my doctor's office. Anyway, my mother and I were asked to sit in the exam room to wait for the doctor. My doctor was an older white man. I really don't know how old he was because I was eight, and all adults seemed old to me. He had gray hair, so he could have been anywhere between fifty and seventy years old. I was not comfortable with my doctor and never liked to be touched or examined. He usually did not talk much to me except to ask relevant medical questions, and I assume my answers were whispers. I remember feeling uncomfortable around him, almost as though he really shouldn't be touching me at all. I somehow knew he was supposed to examine me, but I couldn't help feeling tense. I knew the tension was inappropriate, even as a child, but I couldn't seem to relax.

At this visit, the doctor put the blood pressure cuff on my arm and assessed my blood pressure. He then asked my mother if he could speak with her for a minute in the exam room's waiting area. She said, "OK," and they left the room. I was immediately struck by their leaving after he tested something about my heart, and I knew that asking to speak with her in private was a bad sign. They were talking about my death. My heart was broken, and he had found tangible and solid evidence of the damage. Evidence that my father had broken my heart! I couldn't believe it. On the one hand, I was relieved that finally the evidence showed. The doctor now knew the truth. On the other hand, I was dying. My heart was so broken that the end was coming. I started hyperventilating and crying. My breathing got very shallow and I couldn't catch my breath. I remember gulping for air and some odd sounds coming out of my mouth. I wasn't ready to die. I didn't want to die, and I definitely didn't want to die now that the truth had come out about what my father was doing to his family.

The doctor and my mother must have heard the noises I was making because they ran back into the room with looks of concern on their faces.

My mother said, "What's wrong?"

I shrieked, "Am I dying?!"

The doctor told me that nothing was wrong with my heart but that my blood pressure was a little high and he wanted to ask my mother if everything was OK or if I was concerned about something.

Well, what was I supposed to say to that?

I remember looking at my mom to see if she had said anything, but the tone in the room seemed to strongly suggest that she had told the doctor everything was fine. Perhaps she hinted that I was excitable. I looked at their faces to see if I could get a sense of whether the doctor knew the truth, but it was clear that he didn't know the truth. If he knew the truth, he would have looked at me differently. He would've said something like, "I'm so sorry for all you have been through, and you are so brave and strong."

Instead, he seemed to be thinking, "You are an excitable young child, and I wish you would control yourself."

I suddenly didn't like this situation at all. The car ride home was quiet. It was only two blocks to our home, but the energy in the car was smothering. I wasn't dying and no one was going to stop the situation at home. My mom didn't even seem to care that my body was showing signs of stress. She didn't intervene. This was getting rough. My eight-year-old brain recognized the damage to my heart (MY HEART!), and no one (NO ONE!) was going to help us.

This was bad.

I don't remember if my mom told my dad about my heart condition (slightly elevated blood pressure, heart condition, slow decline toward death, whatever you want to call it). It was never mentioned again. My blood pressure remained slightly high for the next couple of years.

Something happened at least once a month. Mostly the incidents involved my brother and me. My father would become enraged at my brother and I would intervene. My father would beg my forgiveness, and I would grant him mercy. It was a horrible vicious circle in retrospect. I felt that I had to be around or else things would escalate and my brother would die.

It was bad enough that I remember calling home from a sleepover party, begging my mother to come and pick me up. I couldn't tolerate being away in case they needed me.

Friendships

Don't get me wrong, there were a lot of great memories from my childhood too. For example, all I have to do is think of my friend Doozy, and I feel a smile inside my mind. My dad nicknamed her Doozy because she was mischievous. At least that's how I always interpreted the nickname. I don't even know what "Doozy" means. I grew up in a small town and made friends easily. My friends meant everything to me. Doozy lived a couple of houses down from me and moved to our neighborhood from Mexico. She was the middle child of three girls. Her family seemed so different to me. They were so free with laughter. And they were loud. One time, Doozy and I went to the grocery store with her father. She thought one of the boys that stocked items in the produce section was cute, so she started to play with a stack of tomatoes while smiling at him. The tomatoes began to roll off the pile and onto the floor. Her father just rolled his eyes and muttered "loco" while walking away. Her family was very religious and Sundays were dedicated to the Catholic church. I didn't understand the obligations, but realized the church had a sacred presence in their lives. They attended church functions outside mass as well. I'm not sure what these functions were, but one time her mother indicated that she was to bring cookies to a church function. Sounds like my kind of church. Cookies! My friend and I were about ten years old at the time, and we saw this as a magnificent opportunity to demonstrate our competence. We begged and begged and begged her mother to let us make the cookies.

Her mother knew better. She knew we were goofy ten-year-old girls. She doubted our abilities. But we wore her down. I'm sure she acquiesced to get us off her case.

Their home was warm, large, and modern. They had a large, open kitchen. Certain rooms, like the formal living room, were off limits to children. They decorated in style. They were one of the first families I knew brave enough to have white furniture. Most families with children would not have white. Especially with a child nicknamed "Doozy" in the mix.

We were so excited about making the cookies. To accomplish our task, we sat down and made a plan. In order to demonstrate efficiency, we decided to make all four batches of cookies at the same time. Our efficiency would make it so much easier to convince her mother to let us do stuff in the future.

"We should start our own cookie business," we'd tell ourselves.

We pictured her mom telling her friends at church about us and bragging about our entrepreneurial skills.

"My mom's friends are probably going to want to hire us," said my friend.

"We can even make money!" I exclaimed.

We were so astounded by our own capacity to plan a productive business that we set out to prove our skills. We laid all the ingredients out on the counter. This means we set out the flour, baking soda, salt, eight sticks of butter, eight eggs, white and brown sugar, vanilla, chocolate chips, several bowls in several sizes, measuring cups, a hand mixer, measuring spoons, baking sheets, aluminum foil, oven mitts, a spatula, and a wooden spoon. We were feeling good.

We also decided to leave all the cupboard doors open. One of us had the idea that this would help in case we needed to find something in a hurry. The other heard this logic, looked at her friend, and said, "Yes, that's a good idea."

We opened all the doors. We were now prepared.

For each batch of cookies, we needed two and a quarter cups of flour. We measured out nine cups of flour and poured them in a big bowl. The next step was to add baking soda and salt to the flour. Then we mixed.

I was thinking, "This is so easy. I don't even understand why we had to work so hard to convince her mother to let us do it for her. A couple of monkeys could make cookies."

I put the ingredients into the bowl and my friend used the hand mixer to mix the [dry ingredients] together.

I'm not sure which memory is more overpowering: the sight of the flour flying into all the cupboards or the sound of our screaming. The sight was extraordinary. We left every cabinet door open. The mess we made!

Unfortunately, her mother heard us screaming and came running into the kitchen. She was so fashion conscious. She always wore amazing clothes and high heels. I can hear the *click, click, click* of her shoes coming into the kitchen. I can see her face transform into horror as she spied flour spewing all over her kitchen. The torrent of Spanish words that came out of her mouth was amazing. People from Mexico talk really fast. It was the funniest thing I've ever heard. I had one heck of a belly laugh listening to her rant. I think I actually pointed at her while I roared with laughter.

Her eyebrows scrunched up as she looked back at me, a young girl laughing at her disciplining her daughter (and me). I just couldn't understand a word she was saying. She spoke so fast. And in Spanish. I don't understand Spanish. Somehow I associated that family with love and laughter and it never occurred to me to feel unsafe. I could roar with laughter, point at her yelling at me, confident that she would hug me the next day and welcome me back to her home. Even as my friend told me I needed to go home, I giggled. I was polite enough to begin to clean up, but we were not trusted with the cleanup responsibilities.

We did not make the cookies. We were not efficient nor entrepreneurial. My guess is that my friend's mother didn't brag about us. We were a mess. Flour was found in cabinets for months. Had the mixer been in my hand, I would've lifted it up sooner.

I also had boyfriends. Memories of boyfriends bring on a sense of mixed feelings. Our next-door neighbors were a family with four children, three of them boys all around my age. One was my age in school and another was a grade older. The older boy had a crush on me. He was a hockey player and quiet. He didn't speak to me often, even though our families spent quite a bit of time together in the summers. We would drive to a lake and spend the day on their boat. We always had summer block parties in our neighborhood. Our family had a pool in the backyard and people often hung out at our house in the summer. One summer I noticed that when I would swim in my backyard with my friends or brothers, the neighbor boys would watch from one of their bedroom windows. I still don't know whose room that was, but I would often see a head in the window watching me. Once I noticed that, I couldn't help but look to see if it happened again. And it did. Regularly.

I began to notice that this boy had a hard time making eye contact with me. Somehow we began talking on the phone. And eventually we decided to meet one night after dark. I'm sure this was his idea, and my curiosity got the better of me. I met him outside one night and experienced my first kiss. It had hardly happened before I heard my father screaming my name. He was outside looking for me. I was completely surprised he caught me outside. I ran to my house as fast as I could and up the stairs, trying to get to my bedroom.

His hand caught my hand on the banister I used to pull me up the stairs quicker. He caught me and beat the hell out of me. The look on his face is what I see in my head when I think back to that time. He had a look of determination on his face. More like something you might see if you were a log and a logger were trying to chop you into pieces. The arm going up and down so determinedly. I don't remember a single sound, only the look on his face and his arm going up and down. His look was severe. I know that he was angry, but he looked more determined than angry. How someone might look if they found a scary tarantula in their garage and really wanted to make sure it was dead even after they killed it. I had a hard time walking and breathing for the next couple of days.

I was too embarrassed to continue the friendship with my neighbor as well. Clearly I had done something so sinful that it must be totally discontinued. I don't think I even told the boy why. I just stopped talking to him. And I never knew what my dad thought happened out there that night. The truth was somewhat innocent and sweet. Yet my innocence was gone. Whatever message he intended to send me that night, the one I got was that I was bad.

Aside from my father and his violence, our family was normal. There were three children in the family and a dog. My mother did not work. She prepared all our meals, and she and I spent Sundays together cleaning the house. I was responsible for vacuuming, dusting, and cleaning the upstairs bathrooms. My mother did the rest of the cleaning.

I made good grades in school. I had good friends and the teachers liked me. I played sports. My favorite activity was reading. I liked to lie on my bed and read in my bedroom, furnished with a girl's yellow bedroom set. There were teddy bears scattered as pillows on my bed. Our basement was partially finished, which meant we could roller-skate down there with the music blasting (singing our heads off to songs like "I Will Survive" and "My Sharona"). All in all, I would consider myself almost normal.

To cope with stress, I learned to placate. I learned to be helpful and to sit and listen when others were stressed. The world wasn't unsafe, but my father's temper was. To deal with this, I stayed home and made myself available to my family.

Ultimately, I was not successful at achieving this.

TRAUMA: **The Lost Scream**

Many individuals with PTSD have difficulty talking about their traumatic event(s). An individual's ability to tell his or her story can range from extraordinarily detailed to sparse. Some find they vividly remember every detail of the event years later, while others have very few concrete memories. Some set up their lives to revolve around the event (e.g., a victim of rape might begin to work full-time at a shelter for victims of domestic violence), while some avoid associations with their event at all costs. There is no right way to survive a traumatic event. Likewise, there is no right way to share the details of the event. Individuals featured in this book varied in their abilities to share their events. Some were younger when the event occurred, and hence more time had passed. Others had recent experiences. All were brave to tell their stories. This work was difficult to hear, harder to write, and exceptionally painful to share.

I played a lot of different sports during my childhood. You could say that I was athletic but not particularly talented. I did not have the drive to win. I just wanted to play. I played all the typical girl sports except ballet. Instead I was into gymnastics, tennis, softball, volleyball, basketball, track, golf, and swimming. I played to hang out with my friends. I couldn't tell you anything about wins or losses, but I bet I could list who my friends were in each sport.

I think my favorite thing to do in the summer was swim. I swam daily and loved the peace and quiet of it. You know how water feels like oil on your body and you have this sense of weightlessness? That is when you can close your eyes, lie back, feel the summer sun, and let go of worries. Float. And breathe.

My thirteenth summer, I was asked to travel with a group to play tennis. To my surprise, my parents supported the idea. Several coaches were on the trip, along with about fifteen teenagers. The kids ranged in age from thirteen to eighteen. The plan was to travel to different clubs and play in tournaments. Tournament tennis means that brackets are made up for each tournament and players are eliminated by a loss. So the winner of each match would continue to play until he or she reached the championship match. Losers were out. In some tournaments, they would have a loser bracket as well. In this case, losers are transferred down into the loser bracket, and once they lose there, their tournament is over.

If eliminated, we would sit down to watch our friends' matches. When enough of us were eliminated, we would get together and joke around. I remember a lot of laughing and goofing around. Alcohol was also around, and even though I was young, I remember everyone drinking. I'm not familiar enough with tennis tournaments anymore because I don't play them, but I do remember alcohol being a part of the scene.

I suppose I wasn't very competitive, because losing seemed like a fine idea to me. I liked watching my opponent win. That's odd, right? Yet, I liked to watch my opponents win more than I liked to watch them [get] defeated. This is true still to this day. It's complicated, though, because I also don't think I liked the attention associated with winning. It's easier to lose. Then you get to hang out with your friends, cheer them on, make your opponents happy, and drink a beer. What's the problem, right?

I remember one time I was cheering for one of my teammates while sitting in a judge's chair next to the court. These chairs are higher off the ground than a regular chair, so you can view the lines. I had lost already and everyone else was still playing. There was a table with a bunch of food and drinks out for the players. I ignored the food but decided a beer or two was a great idea. I had no food in my system, had played a match out in the summer heat, had alcohol in my system, and was only thirteen years old. And I was probably a little drunk. And it seemed a good idea to me to sit up in that chair and cheer for my friend. So I did. Only it wasn't a good idea. My peers laughed at my antics, but the coaches did not. This was not proper tennis club etiquette.

The guy I was cheering for that day wasn't even much of a friend to me. In fact, I'm not sure I liked him. His name was Bruce. Bruce was from a wealthy family, had blond hair and blue eyes. He was the type of boy that everyone was supposed to like because he had all of those desirable qualities. The thing is that Bruce wasn't the most empathic person I'd ever met. He didn't strike me as someone who had ever suffered in any way. He was unblemished and knew it. Meanwhile I always felt like I had some sort of conspicuous tattoo on my forehead that screamed DAMAGED. And it felt like he knew it.

But the chair was situated on the court he was playing on that day, and for whatever reason, the chair beckoned me to climb up the ladder and cheer him on. Bruce was used to being cheered for, which made it even easier to cheer him on. I was doing what was expected of me. Admittedly I was being obnoxious, but I must have been caught up in the moment of being part of a team. I was a member. I could cheer on a teammate if I wanted and a teammate could cheer for me. It felt great.

Bruce's best friend on the team was one of the nicest boys. They went to high school together and had known each other their whole lives. His name was Kyle. Kyle was the kind of boy that really wanted to know what you were thinking and feeling. He looked directly in your eyes when you spoke, and he asked about you in a genuine way. I don't know how Bruce and Kyle were friends, but that made it easier to cheer Bruce that day as well. He was Kyle's friend. Kyle was the kind of boy you wanted as a friend, but he wasn't a potential boyfriend. He had the look that suggested he was good at math. That's not really fair, I understand. How does someone look good at math? He was smart, attentive, kind, and gentle. He looked good at math. A girl wouldn't look at him and think warrior. They'd think of allergies and pocket protectors. Yet he was very nice and I considered him my friend.

We had been on tour about a month at this point, and I had probably won half my matches. I thought those were pretty good statistics. I had won a couple of matches, lost a couple of matches, and had some fun. My head coach was frustrated by my lack of drive. Looking back at it now, he must've wanted more out of me than I was giving. And to be fair, I probably should've won more matches than I did. But I didn't have that competitive spunk. I wanted to get by. The coaches started talking to me about winning. All of a sudden, I was getting attention. And I did not like it.

Since it seemed important to my coaches that I win more, the day I cheered on Bruce one of the coaches told me I was to come practice with him. The club we were playing at had many outdoor courts and was situated in this beautiful location in the woods. They also had two indoor courts that were not used much during the summer. I could tell that this coach was angry, and I was scared of his anger, but I knew that I had to follow him and try and understand what he was telling me so that I could win more and make them happy.

I hadn't really worked with this coach much. I worked more with the head coach. The head coach was about sixty years old. He was married and his wife did most of the logistics in terms of our housing and movement. He was kind of a cranky guy and serious about tennis. It was business to him. He was not in it for the fun, and I don't remember him laughing much. He yelled and directed. He wasn't mean, necessarily. But he definitely had a direction and a structure to his program. Looking back, I think he wanted to produce tennis players, which was admirable. I don't think I understood him at the time because we didn't have much of a connection. On court, he told me what to do in drills and I did it. He was happy with my performance in practice. He was not happy with my performance in matches.

The other coach was also an older guy. He was probably mid-thirties, overweight by about thirty pounds, loud, and hairy. That might sound unkind, considering I actually liked him as a coach, but it's a fair description of my memory of him. He liked to tease everyone, and therefore he had pretty good relationships with the kids. We could laugh together. He didn't take the business of tennis as seriously as the head coach.

The third coach is the guy I followed that day. I don't really like describing him because the memory of him makes my skin crawl. In fact, I feel like vomiting right now just getting to this part of the story. He was in his early twenties and had blond hair. He was a good tennis player, and either played or wanted to play on the professional tour. Facts about him are sketchy in my memory.

It's also hard for me to recall any specifics of what happened next, except I can tell you the courts were blue. I remember saying to myself that the courts were blue and I remember focusing on them. I told myself to look at the blue-surfaced courts. I know I was raped. I was raped by that coach on a blue-surfaced tennis court the day I cheered Bruce. I was thirteen years old. The entire thing was sudden and violent.

I have absolutely no memory of walking off that court that day. What I do remember was the look that coach gave me afterward. He looked sideways at me. Shame in his eyes. I remember the shame I felt myself, that I had somehow caused him to act like that. A situation that I had tempted and created.

I didn't win another match that summer. And I never told anyone what happened. My behavior got pretty bad the rest of the summer. I stopped talking to people. I wouldn't eat. I had a hard time making eye contact with anyone. That night I stayed with an older couple who lived in a farmhouse in what seemed like the middle of nowhere. That was the longest night of my life. They were an elderly man and woman who lived alone, and apparently offered up their residence to passersby. I spent one night there, but I can remember every detail of that little room. It was a small room, wood-paneled. The bed was in the center of the room and had a bunch of colorful blankets on it. There were a couple of dressers and a smell as though people had lived there for a while. Musty but comfortable. It was the type of home that you could settle in and relax. That was probably because the couple was so friendly. They didn't impose anything on me except they asked me to have soup and bread with them for dinner. I didn't talk much. They gave me pictures of them the next morning so I could remember them. The man had one of those big-mouthed smiles, and I wanted to trust him. He was the social one, and I'm sure it was him that arranged for people to come and stay overnight in their home. She seemed more comfortable at home, making sure there were clean towels and extra bread. We really didn't talk to each other much during my one-night stay, but they were a sanctuary for my penetrated body and spirit.

I sat in that room with a book and tried to read, but I couldn't. Time seemed to tick away so slowly. I was in the middle of nowhere with no one to talk to and nothing to do. I needed distraction. I took an extremely hot and long shower, but it did nothing to cleanse away the dirt. All I felt after the shower was naked. And alone. I knew the entire thing was my fault, but I was having a hard time understanding what I did to create that situation. If my dad tried to kill me over a kiss, what was he going to do to me about this? And most confusing was how to make sure it never happened again. That night was one of the longest nights in my life.

The couple didn't seem to pick up on my dirtiness. They were so friendly, with their pictures and toast and jam for breakfast. The man drove me back to the courts the next day where the team was meeting to ride to our next club. I felt so heavy. It seemed like all of the laughter inside me died.

The head coach noticed my change in attitude immediately. The energy I used to have on the court was gone. Friendliness toward my competitors evaporated. I hung my head and refused to look up. I couldn't eat through the huge cotton ball located in the middle of my throat. Everything tasted dry. It seemed to take an enormous amount of effort to get the food from my mouth to my stomach. The very effort to swallow felt like I was violating myself. The idea of food as nourishment was something that had become completely Greek. Swallowing took energy and felt pointless, particularly with that huge cotton ball stuck in there.

That bad coach left the tour a couple of days later. One day he was there, and the next day I heard he had left. I can only assume that he figured I was about to tell. I wasn't about to tell, though. I didn't want anyone in my whole life to ever know what had happened.

My friends on the tour also seemed to notice a change in me. Maybe it was me, but there suddenly seemed a distance between us where I didn't feel one before. I must've acted odd or removed myself from the group, and they didn't seem to feel comfortable asking me what was wrong. I didn't think they needed to ask because it seemed to me that I had some sort of tattoo stuck to my forehead. A tattoo that read, "Damaged and Dirty." Or one that said, "Yuck." That's how I interpreted their distance from me.

The coaches even got involved to separate me from my friends. The head coach inaccurately assumed that one boy in particular must've hurt my feelings in some way. We weren't dating or anything. Just hung out and laughed at stuff occasionally. He told the head coach that nothing had happened, but he wasn't believed. He was told that if he was seen around me, they would send him home. He told me that and told me he didn't want to go home, so we couldn't be friends anymore. That hurt too. He was the only one that asked me what had happened. I shook my head no as the answer.

SYMPTOMS: **Three Types**

While talking about her trauma, Ren had a faraway look in her eyes. She would not make eye contact with me except when talking about the couple who housed her that night. Her shame was almost tangible, although there were times when I got the feeling she was trying to let herself off the hook. During the entire telling of her story, she didn't even move and just looked off somewhere in the distance. Some people who experience trauma become more comfortable numbing their feelings and work to disconnect from negative emotions. They separate memories and thoughts from their feelings. For many who become skilled at such distancing tactics, healing can only take place when the memories and emotions reunite.

Ren's experience as a child happened almost thirty years ago, yet her recovery and healing started recently.

Individuals with PTSD often experience three types of symptoms. These include reexperiencing symptoms (such as nightmares and intrusive thoughts), avoidance symptoms (e.g., numbing and substance use), and hyperarousal symptoms (an exaggerated startle response and vigilance, to name two).

Reexperiencing

One of the most influential symptoms associated with PTSD is reexperiencing. When individuals have flashbacks, dreams, or intrusive thoughts about their trauma, they often go to great lengths to avoid reexperiencing their trauma. For some, this may mean that they avoid stimuli related to the trauma (in Ren's case, tennis coaches, tennis courts, a specific region of the country, males, and other reminders). Others with PTSD avoid situations that prompt the stimuli (e.g., sleeping). For example, an individual who tends to have nightmares about his or her trauma may develop sleep disorders.

Being raped triggered a series of recurring nightmares for Ren. The context of the nightmares varied, but in each she set herself up as the intended victim of another rape. The nightmares were traumatic for her and resulted in both sleep deprivation and hyperarousal.

Additionally, her perception of self changed as a result of the rape, and she viewed herself as damaged. She believed this was something that anyone could see from her external appearance and functioned accordingly. Thoughts about the rape left her identifying herself as "worthless" and "shameful." These intrusive, shaming thoughts resulted in her hiding from the outside world. She believed she was different from others and could not function normally. To avoid experiencing her shame, she isolated.

Nightmares

Nightmares are awful. Recurring nightmares are awful and annoying. I can't tell when I will have a nightmare, I can't stop it once it starts, and I can't stop thinking about it after I have it.

I have a couple of recurring nightmares. My nightmares involve me being attacked. I wake up before the attack happens but right when it is obvious that my efforts to evade my attacker are going to be unsuccessful. The attack is imminent. I am attacked in my home (with me desperately trying to prevent someone from breaking in) or attacked while on a run (with someone jumping out of a tree in the woods and scaring me). I can never fend off the attacker.

The dream situated within my home involves me being at home and hearing someone trying to break in to get me. The dream starts off innocently. I am home alone, comfortable and content, sitting on the couch in the living room reading a book. I am not worried about anything, and there are no signals that something traumatic is about to happen. The first sign that trouble is on the way starts off with a noise or a movement that comes from outside. Sometimes I would hear something that sounds too close, or I would see a shadow move by the window. I become alert and strain to see or hear more. My heart starts to race and I wonder what I have heard. I sit still and listen for the noise to happen again. It soon becomes apparent that someone is trying to break into my home. I either hear him begin to beat on the door or sometimes see him through a window. I am completely terrified. My mind plays a terrible trick by creating an elaborate door system for him to get through. In this door system, instead of just one door, he has to break through about twenty doors. Each successive door he breaks down is that much closer to me and an attack. There are about five doors already shut to the outside where he is, but I have about fifteen doors inside with me that I can slam to put between us. The worst feeling is when I reach the last door to slam, and I know he has broken through the rest.

I have vivid images of slamming door after door after door, feeling terror, attempting to create barriers between myself and the attacker. I am frightened out of my mind in this dream and would do anything possible to keep him outside. Nothing ever stops him from breaking in, though. I wake up when he gets through that last door.

A typical attack nightmare occurring during a run goes something like this: I am running along a quiet, deserted road. There are not many homes along the road. It is a clear, warm summer day. I am sweaty and hot, with a soft wind blowing up against me and Cyndi Lauper's "True Colors" blaring through my headphones. While running down the street, I don't see any movement, no one in their homes or cars driving by. No dogs barking hello as I run by. Just a quiet, empty street. In the distance, the road rises uphill, hiding the rest of the road ahead. On both sides of the road on this hill are trees. Dense, dark, woodsy trees. It even appears darker looking up ahead toward this hill. I am vigilant, looking for movement. Any movement. Watching for an attack so that I can escape. The attack always takes place, in my dream, at the peak of this hill. Sometimes I will be looking right at a tree and an attacker will slowly come around from behind a tree. I see him. He's always male, but I have no features to give him except male and strong. He is there.

I panic. My heart races and I want to scream "NO!" but it won't come out. I am desperate to get away. The moment he catches me, I wake up.

In the running dream, I am defenseless. There are no cars driving by at that moment, or a house to run to for help. In the house dream, my mind sets up an obstacle of doors. The doors never successfully protect me, but at least I have the doors. Ironically, this serves to prolong my fear.

I should be ecstatic when I wake up from these nightmares because it is just a dream after all. But even when I wake up, it feels like the attack is still imminent. So I sit and listen for sounds. In the night, you can hear many sounds that mimic the sounds an intruder might make. Like the creak of a floorboard. Why does a floorboard creak in the middle of the night anyway if no one steps on it? Does it just serve to frighten children and women? Even the wind blowing outside a window sounds ominous at three in the morning. One time my cat knocked over an empty litter box during the middle of the night, and the sound woke me up and scared me half to death. I didn't get another minute of rest that night.

The middle of the night is a terrible time for the brain because it can come up with so many plausible scenes. Like a phantom has magically transported himself through the door and transformed into a burly, scary man. And now he is holding a bat right outside your bedroom door. He is breathing and waiting for me to go back to sleep so that he can silently pick the lock on the door and come inside. I hear him breathing.

Eventually I realize I have to pee. Sometimes using the restroom is a necessity before I'm feeling confident I'm alone. These times are scary because you have to run, pee, and listen all at the same time you are making a racket and can't hear very well. Plus, you're pretty defenseless when you are sitting on a toilet peeing. I've thought about it and you're doomed.

Once I pee and assess for silence so I can relax, I read. I would spend the rest of the night trying to distract myself from going back to sleep by reading. Sometimes (and these are blissful times) I become so exhausted trying to read and keep myself connected with the story that I have to go back to bed. This is OK because I fall asleep quickly and deeply. Anytime I try to go to sleep before I am thoroughly exhausted, images of the dream come right back and I have to read for longer.

I had a friend once who studied psychoanalysis. She was a survivor of horrible childhood abuse at the hands of her father. She was a lesbian and was kind enough to invite me over for dinner several times with her and her partner. We also would hang out at a lake and swim and hike during the summer. Because she was a therapist and had also been attacked by a man, I was brave enough to share my nightmares with her. I actually thought it was an opportunity to tell someone what had happened to me. I wasn't brave enough to tell her directly, so I thought I could tell her my recurring dreams and then she would magically understand what had happened in my past.

I remember her inviting me over to share dinner. Together, the three of us made some type of vegetarian dinner, and then her partner left for a meeting. I needed this opening to sit with her alone and share my nightmares with her. My heart was beating frantically when I offered to share my nightmares with her. I told her briefly that I had recurring dreams of being attacked *by a man* (I emphasized that so she would be sure to pick up the meaning) while running and in my home. She asked for more details, so I told her about the hill and the doors. I couldn't have been more shocked when she retorted, "Well, that's ridiculous. You're obviously afraid of what's over the next hill and behind the next door. The man is just a symbol of potential evil."

Gasp! Could that be true? I thought I was sharing my trauma. Instead I was waved away as ridiculous and perceived as childishly afraid of the future. It was a long time before I shared my dreams with anyone again. She could be right that I was afraid of the future. But I was terrified of an attack.

Intrusive Thoughts

I think about that day often. Thoughts can be triggered by anything, random things like a dirty bowl in the sink or seeing a cat when I am jogging. Anything associated with my self-worth. The cat reference probably needs explaining.

I lived in a rural town in Florida for about four years. I lived in a two-bedroom townhouse with my brother and we were poor. We didn't have money for socializing or anything, and I kept to myself much of the time. I was going to school then and spent the majority of my time studying or reading. One day someone commented that I wasn't fit. I was mortified and decided to start jogging. Jogging was inexpensive in that you only needed a pair of running shoes. Not necessarily good running shoes, but anything with some cushion.

It became clear on the day of my first jog that the guy was right, I wasn't fit. It took me about half an hour to jog one mile. It was hot and I was slow, nervous, and uncomfortable. I wore those black bicycle shorts, the ones that are tight around your thighs—the kind of bicycle shorts that can make or break a rear end. Some rear ends look great in them, but others just look pitiful. Blubber comes to mind.

What really made me a terrible jogger was my fear of being away from home. I clocked out a mile-and-a-half loop around my house and started to force myself to run the loop twice. This three-mile run would take less than thirty minutes. Not even thirty minutes. It probably took me less than twenty-five minutes, really, given my anxiety about being away from home. I would book through the course as fast as I could so that I could get back to the safety zone of my home. It made me nervous to be out there running on my own away from home, so I would run as fast as I could. Not that first day, though. The first day was slow.

One day, when I was about halfway through my run, a cat jumped from a patch of grass out into the street when I ran by. The cat was white and fluffy and had an attitude problem. It scared the hell out of me. After I screamed and jumped forty feet in the air, I came to a dead stop to look at it (a dead stop was a no-no on my run because I had to get home). The cat looked at me and then slowly walked back into its yard. If real life were like a cartoon, I would swear the cat had a thought bubble appear above its head when it was walking away from me. The thought bubble read, "Dumbass." The cat actually seemed proud of itself for scaring me.

So, the next day when I ran by that house, I looked for the cat in the yard. The cat jumped out of a tree instead. Scared me half to death.

For about two weeks, the cat tormented me. Jumping out from one yard, and then another. From a bush one day, a tree another. I had no idea where to look for the cat anymore. I knew it was smarter than I, and I was frantically looking all over for this cat just so I could see it before it jumped out.

I realized that I had to start "looking" in a different way. I decided to "look" with my eyes straight ahead, but instead of focusing on what was in front of me, I was going to try and see all around me at the same time. Do it! You can look ahead but really be looking all around you at the same time. That's what I decided to do so the stupid cat couldn't get me anymore. And guess what? Stupid cat didn't jump out at me that day. And all because it knew I had figured out how to see it without really looking. That's right! I had outsmarted the cat!

The next day, I went on my run and planned on doing the same thing. When I got to that street, right before that house, I softened my eyes and prepared to "look." The next thing I knew, something had hit me right across the chest, knocking me over onto my back on the street. My first thought was that I was having trouble catching my breath. Whatever hit me had hit me hard enough to knock the wind out of me. My second thought was that the cat and I had collided, and I wondered if the cat was OK. My third thought was the realization (on account of the mailbox situated right over my body) that I had run into a mailbox "looking" for that damn cat. The cat was right. I was a dumbass.

The cat torment lasted for a couple of weeks and triggered terrible anxiety for me. I couldn't differentiate a cat attack from the other attack. I was triggered. And even though I understood I could not be afraid of a white, pompous cat, I couldn't separate my anxiety from the real attack. When something triggers my anxiety, I go into this shutdown mode where I become reclusive. I'm not trying to be reclusive, but instead I'm just trying to recover my equilibrium. It's like recentering.

It takes me a long time to recover. The process can take anywhere between two weeks and a month. When I'm brave enough to venture back out into the world, more or less, there is an additional period of time (a refractory period, so to speak) where I seem to be more fragile than normal. Anything during this vulnerable period can send me reeling back into hiding. Strength seems to be missing from me. Like an infected wound. It takes a period of time for that scab to form, and more time for it to fully heal. Only, I can't seem to heal.

Others don't live this way. Triggered by a cat! You can imagine what happens when I'm triggered by something actually associated with rape. One time, a girl walked by me at about eight thirty in the morning, and she seemed to be drunk. She was swerving and her eyes looked like they were spinning. They couldn't focus on me.

She said, "I need help."

I said, "What happened? What's wrong?"

She said, "I don't know."

We sat down and I waited for her to tell me what had happened.

She said, "I went out last night with my friend and we went to this bar. I like dancing and I remember dancing. I'm not a big drinker and I think I had one drink."

I said, "OK."

She said, "There seems to be time from the night that I don't remember because I start having some fuzzy memories from just awhile ago, and I can see these two guys standing over me and I'm laying in a bed I don't know."

I said, "We need to call the police."

She was like, "Why?"

I said, "What were the two guys doing to you?"

And she started crying. Turned out she was drugged and raped. Spent the rest of the day with the police and at the emergency room having a rape kit done. I have no idea if those guys were caught or prosecuted, but she became extremely promiscuous after that. She told me so herself. She said that she might as well have control over the sex so she figured she'd just hand her body out. It really bothered me. I was reclusive for about three months after that incident.

I avoid news, movies, or books about rape. They bother me, so I keep my distance. But sometimes I'm not prepared for what's going to trigger my thoughts. Like that white cat. It was about that time that movies started to appear about rape. I didn't see any of them, but I remember hearing about them. Like that one with Farrah Fawcett where she was pursued by a rapist. He tried to get into her home. That sounded awful. Not what I would call "entertainment."

Then there was that other movie with Jodie Foster. She was gang-raped in a public place and others watched for fun. She was portrayed as someone who asked for it to happen to her because she drank alcohol and seemed promiscuous. This freaks me out. I don't understand the logic that someone could ask for that to happen to her. Only people who have not been raped could believe that someone asked for it. Classic abuser mentality. "I wouldn't have to hurt you if you didn't make me."

And it's so stupid because there is nothing a person could drink or wear that would make me want to force sex on them. If I saw someone walking around wearing hardly any clothing and watched him drink fourteen beers and six margaritas, I would not be thinking, "Ohh, baby, baby, I would love to have sex with you."

Hell, I would probably run in the other direction.

As can be seen, symptoms of reexperiencing have a traumatic but also dissociative feel. Ren reexperiences her trauma, but in ways that are disconnected from the actual event. Just as she has difficulty remembering the event, some of the details of her reexperiencing are vague. For example, she has immense difficulty describing her attacker. This continues even in her dreams of being attacked. The attacker is vivid for her in his presence and his intention, yet features of his person and the attack are minimized.

Likewise, she secludes herself from society whenever she is

triggered. She describes this as a process of becoming centered. It is probably more accurate to say that she is avoiding being retraumatized. This leads to our next section on avoidance.

Symptoms of avoidance are a cornerstone of PTSD. Feelings of numbness, guilt, depression, and anxiety are marked in someone struggling with PTSD. Individuals may have difficulty remembering the event, such as this victim, and avoid situations that remind them of the event. For many, the use of substances creates an opportunity to further numb emotions and avoid the pain associated with the trauma.

Avoidance

My personality changed after I was attacked. Before I became reclusive, I went through a wild period. I believed my life wasn't worth living anymore and I didn't care what happened to me. I started drinking. I was dirty and damaged. I thought I had done something to cause it. I also thought I had a label smack-dab in the center of my face that everyone could read. Actually, I must've thought people could see the truth in my eyeballs because I had a terrible time making eye contact with people. I thought that if they looked into my eyes, they would see how yucky I was.

So I changed. I no longer played sports. I gained weight. I couldn't have cared less about school or friends or how I looked. I had no hope for the future. I drank.

I drank in the morning, at school, and after school. I didn't see it as a problem because it wasn't every day. And in the morning, it was only a little. But in social situations, it was excessive.

One time, I was drunk enough that my friends locked me in a car while we were at a bonfire party. It was a cold February night in an oceanside town in the Southeast. We tended to gather at each other's houses or the woods for parties. Although we were children, we became experts at breaking into condominiums on the beach. We partied everywhere we could. The only place we didn't gather was on the beach. Police tended to scan the beach for us and move us along. We didn't care to be moved along, so we found other places. My goal for these occasions was to find oblivion.

A couple of my friends locked me in the car that night because I had pushed someone in the bonfire. To be fair, I was too drunk to comprehend what had happened. My brain couldn't process her as a friend. My brain couldn't process fire. And I certainly couldn't put together the idea that fire could hurt someone. I pushed her in the fire because she was interfering with my pathway to oblivion. She tried to take away my alcohol. Perhaps part of my brain did comprehend what I was doing, but it wasn't the very kind part of my brain. I was drunk enough that I had no memory of pushing her, but many observed the scene and verified it as true the next day. Blacking out does not excuse my atrocious behavior, but at the time I believed it did. I was on a path of self-destruction.

So I pushed a friend in the fire because she was trying to get me to stop drinking. To keep me (and others) safe, my friends locked me in a car. On the one hand, this was a brilliant move because I was too drunk to figure out how to open the door (from inside, mind you— meaning it was as easy as opening the door, yet it escaped my abilities). Instead, I kept asking my friends to let me out.

On the other hand, we had been drinking orange soda and vodka (something the owner of the brand-new car I was sitting in knew because she was the one that gave me the drinks). Drunk girls vomit in the backseats of cars.

Orange soda and vodka went into my mouth using plastic cups that we had decorated specifically for the occasion with paint pens, and orange soda and vodka came back out of my mouth during the party inside the brand-new car.

The friend I pushed in the fire that night pursued me at other parties as well. I have a couple of theories about her. She was either determined to save me from abusing alcohol or she was a pain in the ass. I once jumped from a second-story balcony into the marsh to get away from her. I remember some guy yelling about being careful of oyster shells in the water. I could've cut myself up.

People looked out for me. But I was determined. I needed others to see my pain. I needed a way out of pain. I had no clue how to maneuver through the world.

One day I stopped drinking. No, it wasn't just like one day, but one day I became so embarrassed by myself that I could no longer engage in that behavior with any semblance of self-respect. Some type of transformation happened within my brain that associated a drink with humiliation. I looked foolish when I drank. A couple of months later, I started jogging. I suppose I believed then that I was starting to heal. Instead of the obvious and transparent destruction, I was trying to be healthy. But emotionally, I was not better.

Hyperarousal

When the world scares me (which is often), I hide. I hide a lot. I am fearful of people and the things people are capable of doing to other people. There are countless examples of the mean things people do. For example, a father is capable of bashing his daughter's head into the toilet seat when potty training. A father in our community did this very thing. Ended up in prison. His daughter died. His wife went into a severe depression, and his eight-year-old son felt responsible that he wasn't able to get his father's attention away from his sister to beat him instead. That's a mean world, right there. In my worldview, men hurt women and children. Men are capable of cruel acts of violence. Men are also capable of justifying their atrocities with their own special "logic": She made me do it. She knew better than to provoke me.

My own thoughts of the people in the world were scary. So I hid. For years, I checked locks. I checked to make sure I locked my door when I left, and I checked to make sure the door was still locked when I got back. In addition, I checked to make sure no one had snuck in while I was gone. I heard stories of people hiding in closets. So once I was safely locked in, I would check closets and potential hiding spaces to make sure no one was in there with me.

This is an insane way to live. And it feels insane when you're walking around looking for hooligans hiding in closets. The problem is, it's impossible to relax if you don't check. Never check in the first place actually. Because if you walk around and check all the closets, you feel better. And feeling better feels good. And feeling good feels better than feeling anxious. It's just math.

But once you walk around and check that first time, it's over. You become a checker needing that feeling of relaxation that comes after you've checked. Otherwise, you sit on the couch and think, "You're not going to relax until you check and it only takes a minute to check, so just go and check." And you argue with yourself. "No one is hiding in the closet. Why would anyone hide in the closet anyway? You don't have anything worth taking and you locked the door and there is no sign of a break-in."

And you fidget. It's impossible to distract yourself from your own thoughts because your thoughts are right there in your brain and they just keeping wanting you to "check." Just go check and then you can relax. The only thing I am grateful for is that once I checked, I truly could relax. Until I heard a noise. Or left again.

The locks and the checking and the hiding took up a lot of my time. Even though I was aware that all the locks and the checking and the hiding were pathological, there were only a few times when I realized just how bad and different I was. One of those times happened on a bridge in Los Angeles. I was at a Christmas party with friends from work and was driving myself home. I lived in the Los Angeles area for a short time and wasn't familiar with the roads.

For those who have never lived in LA, the roads are complicated. So if I wanted to find my way home from the party, I had to know which street connected with the freeway I needed. And I didn't. Friends from the party told me to take a nearby bridge and find the sign for the freeway. The bridge ended, but there was no sign.

It was around eleven o'clock at night and I was stuck on a bridge in Los Angeles with no idea which road was the right road to take. In other words, I was lost. Los Angeles is a scary place. I had a cell phone and I'm a competent person, or so I told myself, so I pulled over and attempted to dial a friend's number. At this point, I saw a red truck pull over behind me and two huge men step out from each door. I couldn't catch my breath. I couldn't dial. I couldn't even remember the phone number.

One guy came over to the window next to me, and the other guy walked to the passenger window. The guy closest to me said, "Do you need help?"

I panted, "I'm OK."

He repeated, "Do you need help?"

I panted, "I'm OK."

He said, "Where are you trying to go?"

My brain was completely empty. Too busy panting and trying to remember how to breathe.

He repeated, "Where are you trying to go?"

I somehow said, "The Harbor Freeway."

He said, "Follow me."

And they walked back to their truck. Both of them. I was frantically trying to figure out how to get away from them now that they'd walked away, yet I was lost and couldn't find my freeway. I wondered if they just might point me in the right direction. So I followed them. We pulled off onto some highway and were going about sixty-five miles an hour. This lasted for about five minutes. Then we merged onto another highway for another ten minutes. And blissfully I saw a sign for the Harbor Freeway.

I was thinking that I might be able to escape them once I knew where I was going. Of course they could follow me. I was thinking about how much gas I had and whether I could outlast them. Ridiculously, they passed me by and waved. They were friendly. I hid for a month.

Two guys helping out someone stranded in a vehicle in the deep of the night scared me half to death. Something was seriously wrong with me. I should've been grateful. I was grateful, actually, but my fear about what could've happened shut down my functioning for the next month. I needed time to recover from that fifteen-minute experience. That was when I realized how different I am from others. Not in my ability to experience trauma as trauma or fear as fear, but in my ability to recover from the experience. It takes me too long.

The Breaking Point

The breaking point for me happened one random Tuesday. I was driving to work, feeling pretty good. Things weren't spectacular in my life, but everything was OK. In fact, there seemed to be relatively little drama. That Tuesday, I got a call from my daughter's high school. I saw the phone number pop up on my cell phone just as I turned onto the highway going to work. When you turn onto this highway, you leave the small town in which we live. You are in the wider world, so to speak. I remember the location for some bizarre reason, as though it has greater meaning. I left my town to go to work and my daughter's school called. I answered the phone and was told that I was talking to a guidance counselor. That didn't sound so bad. It wasn't the principal. It wasn't the school nurse confirming some horrible diagnosis. I was thinking, "OK, I can handle anything the school guidance counselor has to say."

Even as she talked, I told myself she was full of crap. Drama in a small town. When there is no real drama, people have the opportunity to create drama. So this was one of those instances. Like getting all upset about the vegetable consumption of our teens. I was even thinking, you know, "She doesn't eat enough vegetables, and maybe this guidance counselor business could be a good thing." I was picturing a healthy woman with nutritional charts and a peppy run around the track with her throwing supportive comments at my daughter, like "That spinach made you run zero point zero three percent faster!"

I was on the turnoff now, merging onto the highway, away from my small town. And I shook my head no. No. I would know if that had happened to my daughter. Do-gooders. Everywhere. Surrounding me. There was no need to involve the police because it didn't happen.

It was at this point when it occurred to me that I really would like to check in with my daughter. I called her cell phone and told her what the guidance counselor just told me.

I said, "Is it true?"

Her response was, "Well, yes. It is true."

It took me another fifteen minutes to get to work and be on the phone talking to a policeman. I asked the same question of him that I asked her. "Could this be true? Could that have happened?"

His response was, "This is a really bad guy. He is capable of doing anything. He's a criminal."

It took me several days to breathe normally. What happened to me happened to my daughter. Months ago. And I didn't know.

At home that night, I locked myself in the bathroom with a glass of wine and sank into the hottest bath I could handle. Cried myself stupid. Drank wine. Made decisions. First, I decided that I couldn't kill myself because that wouldn't help my daughter. Unfortunate, because that option seemed appealing. The problem with this idea was picturing my daughter dealing with the grief of losing her mama. This picture was annoying. Children take and take, and then they even take away your suicidal ideation. Parasites. Fine, decision number one was made. No suicide.

Decision number two was to get her some support. So I called every adult woman I knew that cared for my daughter and asked her to send her some love. A card or something to acknowledge her strength. She had the courage to tell and she needed to know that she was not damaged or dirty. She was strong and loved.

Decision number three was to cooperate fully with the police. I carted her off to the stationhouse the next day and had her tell them what happened. She was great. The police were great. They listened to her. The criminal in question was a bad guy and he had done a bad thing and they were going to get him. I liked the math of this equation.

Three decisions made. Actions complete. I thought, "I handled this pretty well. I kept my head in the middle of a terrible situation. Sure, I contemplated suicide, but this option was rejected! I am a good mom!"

I didn't see it coming when the bottom dropped out. The following Wednesday, I come home to a note saying that my husband had left me. He stated that I am unhappy. All of his possessions were gone (he left our child with me). He refused my calls and indicated that it was completely over. I cried for a month. I cried myself into a stupor. Stunned with grief so severe that it's difficult for me to describe. How do you explain that kind of grief? Lasting a month!

No longer was I accepting my "mother of the year" award. I was so consumed with grief that I couldn't focus on her situation at all. Never mind that she couldn't focus at school. Never mind that some of her friends had found out about the case and were being less than supportive. Never mind that she was now focused more on my grief than on her needs as a victim. I was a mess.

And I had taken away suicide as an option.

Recovery: **Take Back the Power**

Individuals with PTSD often ask whether they will ever feel normal again. They want to go back to being the persons they were before the traumas happened. Many seek ways to forget that the experiences ever happened and look for substances that will help them forget. Others attempt to create lives that help them forget the traumas. The key issue here is the purposeful drive to forget. The reality is that they can't undo their experiences. They happened. And they were a part of what took place. Symptoms of avoidance and anxiety or depression commonly follow traumatic experiences.

To work through symptoms of PTSD, it is critical to overcome the "power" of the symptoms of anxiety and avoidance. For example, if someone has severe anxiety about being attacked, it would be important for her to process through that anxiety. By doing so, she takes back her own power over the event. Instead of living each day in fear of another attack, an individual could learn to lower her defenses and radar looking for an attack. An individual overcoming a painful memory could learn to process through her memories so that they are painful but no longer traumatizing. I've talked with many war veterans who speak of the metaphor of watching a horror movie. The first time the movie is watched, it is spooky; but with subsequent viewings, the fear is lessened.

So here's the thing about trauma: Trauma is traumatic. And trauma changes people. It has the ability to change the whole personality. It can change someone from being open and outgoing to being guarded and isolated. A single random traumatic experience lasting one minute can change the way a person sees every second of her life for the rest of her life. That's power.

Fortunately, I believe in the ability to take that power back. In an effort to push away the fear, victims may create a life that is dominated by avoiding trauma. When Ren was traumatized, she hid her trauma and worked very hard to create a life for herself in which she could avoid memories of the trauma. Therefore, she needed to avoid anything that reminded her of the trauma, including the fear. Anything associated with being vulnerable or attacked or unprotected served as a potential trigger for her. Unfortunately, she found that living life meant she was unable to avoid triggers, particularly triggers associated with being vulnerable and unprotected. Because she was unable to avoid them, she developed a tendency or a lifestyle of recovering from having to face potential triggers. She was never assaulted again, but her lifestyle of hiding and seclusion appeared to mimic the behavior of someone who was repeatedly assaulted. Her response to triggers mimicked how she would respond to an actual assault. In reality, she was recovering from the idea of a potential assault.

It's like when you taste something awful. It might even be something you usually like to eat, but one unpleasant taste can make you never want to eat it again. One summer I had a zucchini phase. (Yes, I know, why would anyone have a zucchini phase?) I seemed to love it and ate it almost every night for dinner. One night when I cooked it, it tasted bitter. It was disgusting and inedible. I have not been able to eat zucchini again. Even thinking about it now, my mouth puckers up as if I've tasted something bitter. So the idea of zucchini now makes my brain send out an "ick" signal.

PTSD is like that on a much grander scale. The trauma is so provocative that anything associated with it brings out the same emotional and physical responses. Even though the trigger is not the trauma, the individual may respond as though it is. Life then revolves around avoiding triggers of trauma and recovering from those that cannot be evaded.

When her daughter was attacked, Ren had the opportunity to develop a new response to trauma. Because this experience was so provocative for her, her initial response was to crave the ultimate ending of death. She thought through her suicide in her mind, up to the point of picturing her daughter's grief. She determined that she had to make a choice between suicide, which would cause her daughter more grief, and coping with the present situation. She decided to face the experience head-on. In this way, she was able to put together a couple of adaptive responses to the stressful event. Instead of hiding, she reached out for her daughter. She sought guidance, help, love, and the law from others. She was not able to do this for herself, but she did it for her daughter.

In an unfortunate twist, instead of being able to revel in her accomplishments, Ren encountered more of life's difficulties in the loss of her significant relationship. She had to make the decision whether to continue to seek guidance, help, love, and the law for herself. Ultimately, this proved more difficult for her.

But she did it.

Hope

There is a quote somewhere out there that says something like, "Every adventure begins with a mistake." I made a mistake not talking to someone about what happened to me, and the adventure—life—that followed was half-lived. It is time to start on a new path. I have so thoroughly avoided dealing with that part of my past, even though it still affects me in serious and substantial ways, that I've never experienced my true self or a real life. I need a new adventure. Time to start making things right. Regroup, reorganize, and recover. Decisions must be made.

Perhaps all decisions start with a goal. At the end of my new life adventure, where do I want to end up? I don't know. I certainly don't want to walk around talking about what happened to me as a child. My God, like some crazed [advocate for] child sexual abuse [victims] on speed. Spending hours and hours of my time doing research on the computer trying to find out where the guy lives now, whether he is married or has children, whether he has had any other complaints against him, whether or not he is still playing tennis. Hours more reading into the statute of limitations on women's rights, children's rights, rape, violence. Hours more investigating the best attorneys for litigation. That all sounds frustrating, and honestly I don't see healing at the end of that particular tunnel. It makes me tired to even look down that tunnel.

I also don't see myself becoming a public advocate on the rights of women and children. Cutting up a cardboard box to make a sign that reads, "Stop Violence Against Children," or worse, "I was raped on a blue tennis court and *no one cared.*"

Where would I picket? In front of the perpetrator's house? In front of athletic and tennis clubs? What would I wear? Jeans and a black T-shirt bearing the words "Protect Children" on it? What shoes do women wear to picket? Surely something comfortable. But what exactly? I wonder if the outfit matters. Would other people be more interested in someone wearing formal attire to picket, or can they just throw on sweats? It's hard to imagine picketing when I can't picture the outfit I would wear.

So, I'm not going to do extensive research on litigation, nor do I want to change social policy. What do I want? Do I want my parents to advocate for me, like I did for my daughter? That would be nice, but the idea is ludicrous. I can't imagine telling them what happened to me any more easily than I can imagine driving to work tomorrow in a clown's outfit. I'd more likely work in a clown suit.

What I want most is to be normal. To relax in the idea of safety. To find a happy place inside myself. Accept that it happened to me rather than work so hard to prevent it from happening again or deny it ever happened or believe that I am somehow dirtied and damaged from it. Maybe I want to move on without carrying it around. How does someone find happy? How does someone let go? How do you let go?

I start to look around. Oddly, answers are everywhere. I sit in my young son's room, tears streaming down my face, and a cold yellow washcloth in my hand. He is toddling around the room *vroom vrooming* with a bright red and blue tractor in his hand. There are two skylights in the small room, and from them plenty of light comes in. In one window, a tree stands tall. There are several branches of leaves off the tree, and the branches sway in a way that mesmerizes the eyes. My son would often stare at the branches when lying down for a diaper change.

As I listen to him making tractor noises, feeling the warmth of the sun coming in through the skylights, tears streaming down my cheek, he stops to pick up one of his books. He brings it over to me and says, "Book?" I sigh.

"OK," I say to him, and sit cross-legged so he can sit on my lap. He has brought over a book titled *Owl Moon* by Jane Yolen. I sit and read this book to him, feeling his sweet head next to mine as he points to various animals depicted and identifies them. The last few lines of the book read, "When you go owling you don't need words or warm or anything but hope. . . . The kind of hope that flies on silent wings under a shining Owl Moon."

I think about the concept of hope as my son wants me to read the book to him. Again. And again and again. Hope means that you believe things will be OK. To have hope requires a degree of confidence.

I think of a poem by Ralph Waldo Emerson. I read this phrase years ago and it stuck in my mind: "But in the mud and scum of things— / There alway, alway, something sings."

So how does one maintain hope when things are turning out to be fairly bad? My daughter was assaulted, and that didn't turn out to be entirely tragic. It was wrong on every level, yet she seems to be OK. The law is on her side, the police are on her side, the school is on her side, her family is on her side, and she has a ton of friends supporting her. One can feel a fair degree of hope for her, despite the circumstances.

The person that assaulted her, as well as the one that assaulted me, was a relative stranger. How does one maintain hope when the hurt comes from someone who was supposed to be safe?

I don't know the answer to this question, but little things start to bring me little pleasures. [One] day I went out for a run. I ran about thirteen miles along the river in my town. The path along the river provides plenty of warmth and beauty. A natural opportunity to contemplate concepts like hope, forgiveness, and acceptance. On [that] day, I was thinking about how lucky I was to live where I live. I love the road I was running on. It isn't a special road. It's a two-lane road in a small town where people drive fifty miles an hour going nowhere special. There is only a small shoulder on which to run, and bikers tend to hog it for their own. I love the road. I love the cars speeding by. I love that I know a couple of people who live on the road, so in case I ever have a bathroom emergency, I can knock on their doors and beg for entrance (this has never happened, but it's nice to have fallbacks during bathroom emergencies). I love the river and the reflection of the pine trees in the water. I love the train track along a small part of the river. Every once in a while a small green train will fly by, scaring the absolute hell out of me.

I loved that I had music blaring into my ears so that I could pretend to be various singers. In my own head, I have a beautiful voice. In reality, I am tone deaf and sing like Lucille Ball.

On [that] day, I passed by the eighth mile marker and I saw a beaver close to the edge of the road in the grass. I was happy to see the beaver, as I'd never seen a beaver on the road before. He was fat and cute. He let me get fairly close to him (about six to seven feet away) before he scrambled into the brush. He stuck his head in the brush to hide from me. Unfortunately, [that] particular beaver did not have a good concept of his body because he hid his head so that he couldn't see me, but his butt and tail were still sticking out of the brush. I saw him. He was still fat and cute. I was filled with a feeling of hope out of nowhere.

The beaver hid his head, but I still saw him. This strikes me as a metaphor. Even though you can't see something at the time, it can still be right there. Hope.

A beaver gave me hope? That's pretty cool. I run and contemplate the goodness of a world that will show a girl a beaver's butt just when she needs to see it. I think about everything in my life that is actually going well. Which is almost everything. No, my relationship was not successful, but that did not bring death. Life was still all around me.

I continued to run, glowing in the aftermath of the vision of the beaver's butt when I ran under a tree and a small stick smacked me in the head. A tree released a small stick just when I ran under it, so that the stick fell precisely on the top of my head. The sound must have been something like this: *bonk*. Not a loud bonk. A soft bonk. Almost like a *plunk* sound. I couldn't help but burst out with a smile.

I bless the world that sends me a beaver's butt and follows with a smack on the head. I am sure the stick was a message to not get too comfortable with my hope. Sure, good things come, but they follow with a bonk to the head. It's not all a beaver's butt.

That stick didn't get me down. I kept running.

Happiness

Happiness is all over the place. I walked around gloomy for a month after my husband left me, but I also started to initiate some help for myself. OK, no, I didn't do any of it with a good concept or plan. I was spinning and reeling and crying and wishing for death.

But while I spun and cried, I called friends. My friends called me. About six to eight women checked on me almost daily. At first, our talks were serious and substantial and painful. My friends told me what to do, what decisions to make, how to feel. I doubted everything. They told me it was OK to have doubts. They didn't care about my doubts and told me to act anyway. I was told to call a particular lawyer. I was told how to respond to messages from my ex. My friends got me through days on end by telling me exactly what to do and say. How and when to eat and sleep. It all seemed terribly difficult to me at the time.

My friends were right. They helped me survive during a time when my spirit suffered. For the first time in my life, I relied on others for guidance. Love.

And then there was my family. In my adult years, our family has not been close. I rarely see any of them. It's been fourteen years since I've laid eyes on my father and twenty since I've seen my youngest brother. But I was desperate. So I called for my mother and brother to come and visit me. Help put me back together and hold my head in place, as opposed to the melting that seemed to be taking place. They came. They held me in place. This is happiness.

Happiness comes in all sorts of places. Happiness can even be found in words and phrases. Like the phrase "Don't poke a snake with a short stick." A man with severe depression told me this one day. I asked him, "Why not?" He replied, "You'd be that much closer to the snake." This makes perfect sense and not a lick of sense at the same time. I love it. I mean, honestly, why would anyone poke a snake?

The other day on the news, I heard the general in charge of the war in Afghanistan describing their methods of dealing with a particular region of Afghanistan as "poking a short stick in a hornet's nest." Men and their sticks. Poking them where they clearly should not be poked. I can't really explain the smile that spreads on my face when I hear these phrases, but they make me feel happy. It's easy to imagine a man leaning over a path looking at a snake and saying to his friend, "Hey, grab that there stick over there, will ya? That short one there will do. I want to see if this here li'l fella will move." Picture the friend picking up the short stick and leaning over to his buddy to give it to him. Picture their eyes focused on watching that snake (to make sure it doesn't move before getting poked, mind you). Picture the friend taking the stick, without taking his eyes off the snake, and reaching slowly forward to poke at the snake. Picture the snake jumping at the stick. Both guys jumping back. One declaring, "I'll be!"

Women would not engage in this behavior. If women were hiking and came upon a snake, they would slowly and quietly walk right by the snake without provocation. Neither would ask for a stick to poke at it. And if by any chance, one did declare it a good idea to poke a stick at the snake, the other would introduce reason into the conversation. For sure.

Another phrase that makes me happy is, "I'd rather pop out my eyeballs with forks." The cartoonlike, yet ghoulish, picture is profound. You'd only use this phrase when you really meant it. Like when faced with the prospect of a crowded, noisy grocery store to do a week's worth of shopping with three hungry, demanding children at your side, walking up and down the aisles with the other families, including the grouchy, overweight mother with her whining kids in dirty clothes. Knowing at any moment that mother is going to scream, "Shut your mouth or I'll give you something to cry about" with a growl in her face and eyes that everyone up and down the aisle understands. Eyeballs, forks, pop.

I find happy in a quiet moment outside surrounded by trees breathing in fresh and warm air, hearing the rustle of the wind through the leaves. A hike in the woods. Not even a chatty six-year-old who talks from the time you start the hike until the time you get back home can ruin the peace of a hike in the woods.

I find happy in my daughter's strength. Her ability to connect with animals and to ask for support from her friends. Things aren't going so well in her life, and yet she has support, peace, and love. She cares for me even though she is going through the same thing. She is strong enough to talk to people about what happened to her. And the system pursues justice for her.

I even find happy in sadness. It makes sense that most of us would like to avoid pain. No one signs up to be a rape victim. No one says, "Hey, send me to war so I can personally watch while one of my best friends melts before my eyes." Not many of us would say, "Hey, Mother Nature, please come and destroy everything I've built and all my concrete memories." And it is a good thing we do not instinctively seek out pain and destruction. Those that do may not live long. And they certainly don't contribute to the common good. The feelings that accompany trauma are overwhelming and unpleasant. Painful. At moments, the pain is unbearable. And there is no secret way out, or back door through the pain. It's real and it's staying. The only trick is to still feel joy. To still see beauty in life. It is amazing how often beauty sits there right next to horror.

While my aunt was dying of cancer of the bile duct, my uncle wrote in a mass e-mail to friends and family his experiences of her treatment. He spoke of the suffering in the waiting room and the glaring evidence of illness and death. He also liked to write about those moments of absurdity and strength and fun. In one e-mail he spoke about her sitting in the room having her seventh cycle of chemo-therapy. She was wearing a bright yellow shirt with a multicolored skirt. She was very aware of her fashion choices and needed to be bright and cheery. He was very aware of her strength and his love for her. Her feet became cold, so she asked him to go home and get her "toe socks." Apparently toe socks were a comfort to her. It was important that he brought toe socks that matched her outfit. In the e-mail, he spoke of how difficult it was to still feel like a man when he was sent on a mission to find toe socks that matched a particular outfit. He was successful on several counts. His mission to get her toe socks brought her comfort and love when [she] desperately needed [them]. His mission to get her toe socks brought another patient a moment of reprieve because she smiled. And his sharing of the mission gave every reader a glimpse of love. Beauty and horror. Side by side. Which one we attend to is our choice at every given moment.

So the trick for me, the transformation, will be to find happy in my trauma. To re-create it so I am OK. So that I can see the beauty next to the horror.

Forgiveness

I've thought a lot about forgiveness, more about acceptance. I've spent the majority of my time and energy focusing on making sure I am safe. Essentially, this has led me to a life of looking for things that could possibly go wrong. And when things do go wrong, I blame both the situation and myself. In other words, my life is misery.

Here is an example. My husband was the type of person that was always aware of how others perceived him. Their acceptance of him was of utmost importance. To him. Therefore, while I am hyper-focused on issues of safety, he was hyperfocused on issues of accep-tance. There were times when those needs conflicted. Such as during introductions. When introducing me to a male friend or colleague, he tended to introduce me as his wife and used all sorts of complimen-tary words regarding my work or role as his wife. When introducing me to a female friend or colleague, I was typically introduced with my full formal name. An introduction to a new female colleague went as follows.

I was walking in to work after having spent the last couple of hours at a meeting across town. I walked in through the front doors and turned to the left to go down the hallway where my office is situated at the end of the hall. Usually this hallway is bare. On this day, I looked to see him standing in the hallway peering into a newly occupied office. He was smiling and happy. I wondered what on earth had made him so jovial, as that does not tend to be his mood at work. As I walked by, he put a hand on my arm and said, "I would like to introduce you to some people."

I looked over and saw two women standing inside the office. I noticed that there were two desks in the office. I smiled and waited.

He said, "This is Linda and this is Rachel."

One was an older woman, approximately fifty, wearing black slacks and a peasant top. She smiled and said, "Hello." I got a good vibe from her. She seemed pleasant, competent.

The other woman was younger, approximately twenty-five, wearing black slacks and a gray blouse. She smiled and said, "Hello." I got a good vibe from her. She seemed pleased.

I said hello back to both of them and turned to walk toward my office. This is when he said, "She is the woman who works down at the end of this hall."

Well, Christ Almighty. I felt my shoulder pinch upward and my jaw clamp shut. I turned and looked back at him with what could only be a shocked (slightly perturbed) look on my face. The woman who works down the hall? Seriously? What the hell was that? What woman wants to be introduced by her husband as the woman who works down the hall? I was not having my most flattering moment.

I sat at my desk and breathed a couple of deep breaths. My first thought was that he would be turning into my office any second now and taking back his hideous introduction. Telling me that he had just been talking about me and describing my work and how lucky he was to be married to me. Except he did not walk into my office. OK, fine then. Maybe there were other explanations for his behavior.

Maybe he was attracted to the women and did not want them to know he was already involved with someone else at work. If this explanation were true, he is a rat. But a rat is a rat, so he should be free to be a rat and either or both women were welcome to him.

Maybe he had poor social skills. If this explanation were true— well, it's not true actually. He has relatively good social skills and tends to be keenly aware of how to make people comfortable.

Maybe he has had the unfortunate experience of introducing two women to each other before, having relations with both of them, and therefore developed a habit of introducing women without reference to their relation to him. If this explanation were true, he is a rat. A rat is a rat and can only be a rat. Exit me, welcome them.

Maybe he is a slow learner, as we have had this type of occurrence come up in our relationship before and he continues to engage in the same behavior. If this explanation were true, it would also be true that I am a slow learner. Since we have had this occurrence before, it would generally be I that am the slow learner. He displayed his behavior from the beginning and I wished for it to change. When it did not, I needed to accept his "ratness."

None of these explanations are particularly appealing.

When we did interact, he admitted it was "old behavior" of needing "to keep his options open." He admitted that he was wrong to have behaved like that and that he wouldn't do it again. He apologized and stated that it would not happen again. Again.

Forgiveness would mean that I accept his apology and let it go. I know there are many people who would hear this story and roll their eyes, thinking, "Give it up, chick. He's a player." Yes, he is a player.

To not forgive would mean that I continually say to myself, "He hurts me. He takes me for granted. He is not to be trusted." This is misery.

Every time I say this to myself, I bring hurt into my life. I don't wish to have the hurt in my life.

For today, I choose to instead think that he has poor social skills when it comes to introducing women to his wife. He has poor self-esteem and craves attention from women in order to feel good about himself. There is nothing about this that is admirable. Who would want to be the person who constantly works to make others like him? I feel sad for him.

Feeling sad for him doesn't mean he has permission to treat me like that. Instead it means I hope for more for him. I hope he is able to see his own strengths and greatness and doesn't need to hear it from others so much. I hope he is able to look at himself in the mirror and feel good. Sure, it feels good to hear someone else thinks you are good. But it feels great to look at yourself and have confidence. Because when push comes to shove and things get rough, you've only got yourself as backup. And if you're not up to the challenge of life, you will feel misery.

Will he hurt me like this again? Maybe. But then again, maybe not.

Forgiveness means that I am able to see the world the way I would like to see it. And I would like to see the world and the people in it as benevolent. Yes, sometimes people make terrible mistakes. But we are all just people. Perhaps in the end, we are all looking for the same thing.

Acceptance

To accept my experience means that I have to transform what I have always viewed as dirty and damaging into something less traumatic. It could be as easy as tweaking my perceptions. It could be as hard as tweaking my perceptions. I could tweak my perception of dirt, for example. I viewed the experience as something that dirtied and scarred me. Something that anyone could see if they just looked at me. In reality, no one ever even guessed what happened to me that summer day when I was thirteen.

On the other hand, I could decide to view the experience as just dirt. Just as if I went and played at the park that day and got filthy dirty. I could have come home and washed it off. Instead, I worked hard to reapply the dirt into my image every day from there on. Now, that's ridiculous. I don't want the dirt.

Instead, I can use different images to wipe the dirt from my mind. It happened to me, and yes, occasionally it still gets me down. But I have different ways of coping with the experience now. Instead of letting that dirt seep in, today I choose to clean it off. Breathe it out. Apply something more cleansing instead.

Relationships and Outlook Today

I am new to my recovery. I have good days and bad days. I have days when I can apply what I've learned and I feel much happier. Ironically, giving up control over my safety results in me feeling safer. I never would've guessed that years ago. Yet, I don't have to look around and see all the potential dangers. It's exhausting to be on the constant lookout for danger. And because I'm not looking for all those dangers, I feel safer.

As for my bad days, well, I have bad days. But it's just a bad day. It's not dirt.

My new outlook on life means that I believe certain things:

1. **I have to let go of hurt.**

   Holding on to the hurt means that I continue to hurt. I give power to the hurt by keeping it close to my heart and soul. I don't want the hurt as part of my heart and soul anymore. Instead, I want happiness, forgiveness, acceptance, and hope.

2. **I have to accept that people do bad things.**

   People do bad things sometimes. Yet six or seven other people are waiting right there to pick a person back up. Odds are better that people are good.

3. I make mistakes.

And sometimes these are the memories we cherish for life. Like my atrocious cookie-making skills as a child, or the time I ran a marathon with bronchitis and passed out at mile marker seventeen. While the paramedic applied logic ("Hey, lady, don't run marathons when you've taken cold medicine every day for the past three weeks. You're dehydrated and it's a ninety-degree, humid day today."), my friend applied the support when I was dropped off at the finish line. She cried with me. Sometimes failure is a precious and beautiful thing.

4. Life is worth living.

The meaning you give to life is something you can constantly reevaluate for yourself every day. For myself, I am focused on hope. Today.

CHAPTER 2

Beads: Hershel's Story

BEFORE TRAUMA: **Color Blind**

I NEVER THOUGHT ABOUT what a hero was until I actually met one. Prior to meeting Hershel, a hero to me resembled a cartoonlike character that happened to be in the right place at the right time and would save someone who was in a vulnerable position, such as an elderly woman crossing the street who was just about to get hit by a runaway car. The surrealistic superhero whisks the woman out of harm's way and holds her in his arms while he checks to see that she is OK. The act of bravery would result in smiles and cheers all around. Importantly, I believed that acts of heroism were lucky accidents—something any one of us would do in the same situation. Any one of us would have behaved the same way, but the scenario presented itself precisely to the lucky one who happened to be standing right there. A fellow passes by while a girl is trying to get her cat out of a tree, so he hops over the fence into her yard, climbs the tree, and rescues the cat for her.

Bravo! Cheers and applause.

Or, a fellow is down on his luck and struggling financially, yet he turns in to the local police station a wallet full of cash that he found on a sidewalk. Kudos!

As far as I could tell, such acts were really just about lucky chances to be a hero, and anyone could do them. And since anyone could be a hero on any particular day, given the right circumstances, the notion of heroism really wasn't that interesting to me. Someone was presented the opportunity to behave in a heroic way, and he took it. Ho hum.

I now know I was wrong. Acts of kindness and behaving heroically have nothing to do with luck. A hero is not made by opportunity. A hero is inside the spirit. A hero acts in the face of despair. Being a hero hurts.

Heroes don't walk away smiling, soaking up the applause. Heroes walk away with nightmares; they are sometimes even scarred and bruised. When you first meet Hershel, you might not know he was a hero. He certainly wouldn't be the one to tell you. His mannerisms suggest a cross between Eeyore and Forrest Gump. Your first thought might be that Hershel has severe depression. His voice is deep and strong, but it sounds beaten down and heavy. He speaks with a slow Southern accent and sounds hopeless. He does not talk about his future, except in terms of how to shorten it or make it somehow endurable by escaping the presence of other people. He speaks of his pain and his efforts to tolerate his life. The word "done" is frequently and forcibly vocalized.

You might feel concerned. He sounds suicidal. Is this individual at imminent risk of taking his own life? His words and mannerisms would suggest yes. Yes, in fact, he is contemplating his death. The only thing is, Hershel is contemplating a hero's death. And it is not his time.

I was not popular. I didn't have a lot of friends growing up. We lived on the bad side of town. My mom worried about sending me to school on our side of town, so she sent me to a private school on the other side of town. Rich kids go to private schools, and we were not rich. Because of this, I was picked on a lot. I didn't have the right friends or clothes or family.

Because I didn't go to school with any of the kids that lived by me, I didn't have anyone to hang out with after school. So I read a lot. We didn't really have any books, so instead I'd read the encyclopedia. I spent a lot of time reading the encyclopedia from back to front.

I'm chock full of useless knowledge. For example, I know a lot about Vikings. Not the football team, but the real Vikings. Did you know that axes were considered the main battle weapon? They preferred hand weapons to weapons that were used from a distance, like bows. Also, the Vikings didn't really have horns on their helmets like people believe today. History wrote [about] them as barbarians, but they weren't like that.

I also like to take things apart and build them back up. My mom dated this guy for a couple of years who taught me how to tear down and build up a motorcycle. When I was old enough to get my first car, I stripped it down and built it back up with his help. Those were pretty good days. I learned how to see each part as its own piece and how each piece worked on its own, but also how it all got put back together as a whole. It's important that a piece serve its purpose in the overall whole.

My mom and dad divorced when I was three years old. I got to spend every other weekend with him. We'd go fishing a lot. And play board games. Operation and Battleship. He was real good at model rockets, so we'd build one of them and fire it off. When I got older, he came to my football games.

I got pretty big in school. You'd guess that would be a good thing since I got picked on a lot, but it didn't help me much, except in football. Though big, I didn't like to fight. Even if some kid hit me, I'd let him hit me and just move on. My mom told me once that if I didn't fight back, she'd whip me after school. So I punched this kid in the mouth when he called me fat. Punched out his two front teeth. My mom didn't whip me that night, but I sure felt bad about it. I know he deserved it and all, but it didn't feel good. People are seriously hurt all over the place. I don't need to add more pain.

My dad had degenerative joint disease. Had about thirty-five sur-geries, including ten on his back, others for his neck, shoulders, knees. He was always in a lot of pain.

He died from a massive coronary when I was seventeen years old. They said that during his last minutes, he wasn't in any pain at all on account of the anesthesia. I'm glad he went like that. I hate all the pain.

The week my dad died was the worst week of my life. Monday of that week, I was told by our doctor that I had pneumonia. On Tuesday, my mom went in for back surgery and I was left with my stepdad. Me and him didn't get on too good. My mom and I would talk about things, but he would try and interfere.

Like one day, I decided that I didn't want to go to school. I lay in bed that morning instead of getting up to eat breakfast. I didn't pull on my jeans or brush my teeth or anything. Just lay there. So my mom came in my room and said, "What's wrong?"

I said, "I don't want to go to school today."

"Why not?"

"I don't feel real good," I said.

She stood there looking at me for a second or two. I kept my eyes closed, but I could tell she was looking at me. She said, "Well, lie in bed and relax so you feel better." She walked over to the bed, put a hand on my head, and lightly ruffled my hair.

"Yes ma'am," I replied, keeping my eyes closed and resting into the pillow. I didn't really feel sick, but I didn't want to go to school. Having my mom touch me felt good. Like I really was sick and her touch helped me feel better.

For the next ten minutes, I lay there and took long, deep breaths. For that day, things were going to be OK. I was at home. I could rest. I could be there the whole day. No one was going to pressure me or make fun of me or give me crap. I could just sit right there in bed and breathe. It felt good to just lie there. I didn't even have to think.

I barely even noticed that time had gone by even though I was pretty sure I heard my mom's car back out of the driveway to head to work. Might've even dozed off for a second. I woke up when I heard my stepdad come in my room and bark, "Get your ass outta that bed and get to school!" I didn't answer him. What the fuck did I care what he wanted me to do? Didn't take but a second for him to grab my legs and try and pull me outta bed. "What are you doing? Me and my mom already talked about this and I'm staying home."

"Damn you are. Get to school," he yelled back at me. I hated his face. Right then, he had it all snarled up like I was some kinda dog he wanted to beat. Eyes all crazy looking like he wanted to shoot darts out of them right through me. We got in a bit of a fight until I grabbed a baseball and threw it at his face. Missed a little and it went into the wall.

We didn't talk after that and I didn't go to school. Put me in a bad mood too. Me and my mom had things on good terms, and he just came in and ruined everything. So when my mom went off to have her back surgery that Tuesday, I was left with this asshole. He didn't care nothing about me.

The very next day, my dad died of a massive coronary. On Monday, I got pneumonia. On Tuesday, my mom had back surgery. On Wednesday, my dad died. It was a bad week. Like the saying goes, "When it rains, it pours." I believe that too. Put it on the list of rules. (Rule number five: When it rains, it pours.) I'll tell you about the other rules later.

Back to that bad week. On Thursday of that week, our opponents in the football game for Friday night sent our team some flowers. The card with the flowers read, "These aren't for your dad, they're for you 'cause we'll be attending your funeral after the game tomorrow night." Well, that pissed me off bad. I was a big defensive end for our team and I was pissed. On the first play of the game, I took out the opposing quarterback. I spent the whole game tackling. Tackling hard. Hurting and ready to do some damage.

My life changed a little after that week. My dad wasn't around and I didn't want to be around my house. So I didn't spend much time at home. To be honest, and I'm sorry to have to admit this, I spent the rest of my senior year drinking. I spent time over at a friend's playing paintball and drinking. Nothing else made sense to me.

My mom and stepdad divorced shortly after her back surgery. She is the type of person that when she gets mad, she just needs a little time to chill out and calm her feelings down. I've always known that about her. She just needs a little time and then everything will be OK. But if you bother her before she is ready to talk, it's bad. She's not ready. So my mom and stepdad were fighting one day and she was trying to get out of the house and away from him. He wasn't listening and was trying to pull her back to talk to him some more. He wasn't listening that she needed a moment to calm back down. When she tried to walk out the door, he grabbed her arm and pulled her back.

I said, "Let go or I'll snap your neck."

He gave me a look like he was ready to have a go at me as well, so I punched him right in the face. Broke his nose.

They divorced soon after that. (See rule number fifteen: Good idea to give a person some time when they are mad at you before aggravating them some more.) Never mind. I'll tell you more about the rules in a little while.

The Army

I join the army because I want to do something different with my life. Something better than what I am doing. It's not that I don't like what I am doing. In fact, it's all right and I am good at it. But I want to learn more and be more. The United States Army could teach me a lot. Like a lot of people, I sign up in 2001. But I sign up before September 11.

On September 11, I am heading out to buy my mom a birthday present and as I'm about to go out the door, someone yells to come and look what is on the television. Broadcasts of the towers coming down. I think, "Uh oh. I'm in the army now, so I suspect we're going to be asked to do something about this."

Basic training is good. The first part goes just like what I expect. The drill sergeants don't like the piercings I have and give me hell about them. I don't know why. I take all [the rings] out because I know I can't have them in the army, but who cares about the holes? For some reason, they see them as reason to attack me. Like I'm some kind of hippie. I'm not a hippie. The first time a drill sergeant calls me a hippie, I turn around and say, "Excuse me, drill sergeant, but would a hippie do this?" I stick my finger up my nose.

I have to do a lot of push-ups in basic. But at least in the army, you know the drill sergeants are screaming at you for a reason.

A typical day in basic goes something like this:

4:30 a.m.: Wake up.
5:00 a.m.: Outside stretching.
5:30 a.m.: PT. Running, push-ups, sit-ups, etc.
6:30 a.m.: Shower and put on your BDU [battle dress uniform]. Meet for roll call formation.
7:30 a.m.: Mess hall for breakfast.
8:30 a.m.: All-day trainings.

I like it. I like some of the trainings more than others, though. On account of a knee injury, I'm in basic for a year and have to do a bunch of physical therapy. In the marines, you are assigned a job. In the army, you pick a job and sign a contract. I want linguistics and coding. Of course, I don't get linguistics and coding because the stupid eye guy says I'm color blind. I'm not color blind.

It's one of those long-ass, boring days where you just have to go from one line to another and complete assigned tasks. I don't mind the tasks, really. It's just going from one to the next and standing around a lot. I wear glasses and contacts and take out my contact lenses for the eye test. This confirms that I need glasses and contacts.

The next part is to confirm color vision. So I ask this guy if I can put my contacts back in.

He says, "Nope." Doesn't even look up or anything. Just says no.

I wonder how I'm supposed to see anything when I can't see anything. So I say, "I can't see anything."

He says, "What color is this?" and points in some direction. I can't see where he's pointing to because I can't see without my contacts, so I say, "I can't see without my contacts."

He says, "I guess you are color blind."

I contest this, of course. You can't go into linguistics if you are color blind. So they are nice enough to get me an appointment the next day for another color vision test. I walk in that room, feeling determined to set the record straight. I walk in and see this guy sitting in an office. He's already got a look on his face like he's annoyed that I'm in there. I say, "I need to get another color-blind test because I'm not color blind."

He says, "What color is my shirt?"

I say, "Green."

He says, "What color is this folder?"

I say, "Red."

He says, "Congratulations, you are not color blind."

That night I am feeling relieved and hang out with some buddies to go to a bar. I'm just happy that I can go into linguistics and coding, because it's what I want to do. We drink some beer and I'm relieved that all the tests are over. Now we can start doing some more focused training for our particular jobs.

The next day, I find out that I am still considered color blind. It is acknowledged that I have green-red vision but am still color blind. Really? So I can't go into linguistics. I can be either an MP or an engineer. What kind of logic is that anyway? I can't read words, but I can play with different colored wires. Military logic.

I sign on to be an MP. I ask to be stationed in Korea. No one gets turned down for Korea. They turn me down for Korea. I ask to be stationed in Germany then. I am turned down for Germany. I ask to be stationed at one fort. I receive orders to report to another. Effective immediately.

Welcome to the army. The funny thing is, it's not that horrible.

Training

My favorite stuff from basic training was the outside, hands-on stuff. The bayonet course was good, and so were the team-building courses. You had to think outside the box.

The bayonet course got my adrenaline going. They would set up an obstacle course that we would go through. The bayonets were made to look like M16s, and had an eight- or nine-inch metal spike. Dummies were set up throughout the course for us to hit. Dummies were really tires and plywood, but that don't matter much when you have drill sergeants barking at you. The dummies were the "enemy" and we had to strike them. We would crawl on our bellies or run up and hit the dummy with one strike. The one hit would represent what it would be like to be in a knife attack with only one shot at an enemy. The last dummy set up on the course was the dummy you were supposed to hit for twenty seconds. This represented a longer knife fight in battle.

The problem was that by the time you got to that last dummy, your adrenaline was so high. My adrenaline was so high that my bayonet got stuck. I stuck it in way too far and couldn't get it back out. So I was standing there in front of my dummy with my bayonet way inside of it, and I was trying to pull it out during my twenty seconds. I was pulling and pulling, but couldn't get it back out. Two drill sergeants were standing off to the side of me, laughing.

One said, "You don't mess around, do you, pal?"

The other chuckled and said, "The one-shot-only principle applies to a gun, not stabbing, son."

I think I was pretty good on the bayonet course. Before we left for war, one of my commanders asked me what I thought about going over there. I said, "I want to get this done so I can get back."

He said back to me, "That's the best answer I've heard all day."

I have to admit, I was pretty nervous about going over there.

TRAUMA: **Being a Hero Hurts**

Once we got to war, there were times when there was a lot to do and times when it was just monotonous. Some days would go by so fast, and you didn't have any time to think. Other days, especially those days full of driving, you might have too many thoughts rolling around in your brain. To be honest, I didn't care much for all that time to think about things, but I also realized that I better have a system to survive. A system of rules, so to speak. There were certain rules of war that I was going to live by. Some of the rules were basic rules of war, but others were my rules of war. I had to live by them or else I was going to die. Or worse, I could hurt someone else.

Here is my list of rules of war:

1. Don't kill women and children.
2. Treat your enemy with respect.
3. Don't get yourself killed.
4. Do what you are told.
5. When it rains, it pours.
6. Real war ain't like a video game.
7. Sleep is good.
8. Don't burn anything near grass.
9. When someone points a grenade machine gun at you, back off.
10. When someone points a nine millimeter at you, back off.
11. Don't stay in your vehicle when mortars are incoming.
12. Spread out (sixty yards apart).
13. Depress into the ground so you are not hit by shrapnel.
14. Mess hall food is better than MREs.
15. Give a person time to calm down before talking with him.

These are my rules of war. I can explain some of them, if you would like. For example, rule number two: Treat your enemy with respect.

In war, information is good. To gather information, we talked to locals and suspected terrorists all the time in order to get more information. Therefore, if we captured an enemy or a suspect, it was important to keep him alive so that he could give you more information. If you capture someone, he is your captive. You don't treat him bad, because now he is your ally. He is now set up to help you accomplish your mission, so you need to respect that person.

I've had several opportunities to test this rule. For the most part, I kept up my end of the bargain, although there was one time in particular this wasn't tested because we didn't capture the person I wanted to capture. I would say, in that instance, it was probably a good thing that he was not found.

We had several suspected bombers in our care. One day the interrogators needed a break, so they asked us to take over. We were specifically told "not to break the Geneva Convention."

We didn't break the Geneva Convention, but we also needed to set up the captives in a position so that they were more likely to give us information. To do that, several things can be done. One useful tactic is sleep deprivation. It's suggested that captives are deprived of sleep for forty-eight to seventy-two hours. This helps them be in more of a position to talk to you.

So these captives were not allowed to go to sleep. I was only in there with them for two and a half hours, but I was up to the task of keeping them awake. I was good at my job. I kept them awake. What I did was a bunch of PT. That means you ask them to walk back and forth carrying sandbags, or have them walk with five-gallon jugs of water, or ask them to do sit-ups and push-ups. Nothing a good football player wouldn't love doing, but I think when you are sleep deprived and held captive by the enemy, maybe it's not particularly fun for them. I knew they were working hard because one of them drank some water and threw it right back up. That's evidence of a pretty good workout.

You might think I would have made a good interrogator, and one of the interrogators said just that. But I wouldn't have made a good interrogator. To be a good interrogator, you have to be detached. And I wasn't detached. I cared.

In fact, I was feeling rage.

Even though I had them going through some PT, I was nice to them. I said thank you. I even said please.

Rule number three: Don't get yourself killed. Really? Anyone think I need to explain that one?

Rule number four: Do what you are told. There were a couple of female soldiers in our platoon. That was fine really, but we had one in our platoon that was very good at being an MP. She knew the rules and everything. She was good at law enforcement. Problem was, she didn't think MPs went to battle. When she was in the field, she was lost.

One time, mortars started dropping on us and we started taking direct fire. Rules are that you don't stay with your vehicle. You spread out and depress yourself into the ground so that you are not hit by shrapnel (rules eleven, twelve, thirteen). Well, she started screaming and crying and wouldn't get out of the vehicle. I was looking at her, thinking she was not following the rules and she was going to get herself killed. So I grabbed her and tried to pull her out of the Humvee. She was screaming and crying and holding on to the vehicle, and I was thinking she was crazy. So I pulled her legs and grabbed ahold of her so I could move her away from there. I didn't care that it put me at risk, but she could have gotten herself killed.

I screamed to her, "I understand this is stressful! Do what you are told!"

She was clinging to me and I had ahold of her legs and body while I ran away from the vehicle. I heard her crying.

I screamed, "Depress yourself into the ground so you don't get hit by shrapnel! You are a soldier, act like one!"

I put her on the ground, looked her in the eyes, and said, "If you need me, I will be sixty yards in that direction." I pointed due north of where she was lying on the ground.

She could've gotten herself killed.

Rule number seven: Sleep is good. Nine thirty or ten o'clock was bedtime. Sleep was good because it meant there was less time to think about everything. Don't see that I need to say anything else about that rule. It should be fairly self-explanatory. Sleep is pretty much useful on any given day. So if you can get a good night's sleep in the middle of a war zone, well, that's just bonus.

Rule number eight: Don't burn anything near grass. When not on convoy, we got to do fun stuff like burning trash and feces from the portable latrines. We would burn feces in fifty-five-gallon drums that are about one [yard] tall. Gas is poured in (jet fuel really). The contents of the drum are mixed and then you throw in one match.

Crap-burning duty lasts for two days and only gets complicated if it's windy. On windy days, you have to line the drums up next to each other so that if you light one barrel, the ones next to it also light.

Also, you only light jet fuel up if you are in the sand. Grass catches fire quickly. One time an ember hit a grass field and the whole field caught on fire. The fire went to a warehouse housing a cache of explosives. Mortar rounds, rocket-propelled grenades, artillery rounds. You could hear all of those going off when the fire got into the warehouse.

That was when we figured out that you could only burn things on the sand. It don't catch fire quite so easily.

All of these war games that people are playing back at home don't include crap-burning detail or trying to take a crap in the middle of a sandstorm when you can't find your way over to the portables. (Rule number six: Real war ain't like a video game.) One time I had to go right by the trucks. Never saw that in one of the war games. What would you do if you were standing there in the middle of a sandstorm and couldn't even see your fingers in front of your face? If you can't see where you are walking, then you can't get to where you're going. And if you're going to take a crap, you have to see where you're going. Otherwise, you just have to drop them right there next to the truck. It ain't right.

Rule number nine: When someone points a grenade machine gun at you, back off. Convoy missions are not fun. They are a pain in the ass. In Iraq, we would usually spend two weeks doing convoys and then one week doing security patrol. A typical convoy meant that we would drive hours to our destination, wait for our pickup, and then turn around and escort our pickup back to the base and do the handoff.

We did a lot of driving and waiting during convoys. We would eat MREs on the road and hope to get back in time to eat at the mess hall. (Rule number fourteen: Mess hall food is better than MREs.) If you don't know what an MRE is, it's an army meal that is ready to eat. It comes in a plasticlike bag the size of a brick and has all the components of a ready-made meal. You can get all sorts of food in an MRE, even vegetarian options like a bean-and-rice burrito. The thing about MREs is that they start to all taste alike on the battlefield. Hard to tell whether you are eating a bean-and-rice burrito or chicken tetrazzini after you've eaten so many of them. Lots of guys stockpile MREs back at home. They might be handy in an emergency, even though they don't taste so good. But I'll tell you what, I'd take an MRE over being hungry any day.

One squad would go on a convoy, about ten people. My job was the gunner on the rear security vehicle. I waved vehicles off that got too close. If they wouldn't back up, I would point a weapon at them. The Mark Nineteen is a grenade machine gun with a barrel as big [around] as a golf ball. The Mark Nineteen is going to do some damage. If a vehicle didn't back off when this was pointed in its direction, sometimes I would pull out my nine millimeter.

Astounding. A big barrel looking right at them, and they wouldn't flinch. But then I pointed a little nine millimeter at them and they would freak out and hold their hands up off the steering wheel with an expression on their faces like, "OK, OK." Really? You wouldn't back off with a grenade machine gun looking at you but the nine millimeter . . . ?

It's important that other people understand these rules, I think.

Rule number ten: When someone points a nine millimeter at you, back off. (This is similar to rule number nine regarding grenade launchers, yet it seems like people need the differentiation.)

Back at the base, I would do security patrol. This meant that I was up in the turret ensuring that only certain vehicles came through the checkpoint. This was my job. Remember that I'm military police. So when someone tries to come through anyway, my job is to wave him off. If he stills tries to come forward, I have to pull out my nine millimeter. If he continues to try and move forward, I shoot. One time this Mercedes pulled up. The driver was told to stop and he didn't. So I shot off two rounds. One landed in front of the vehicle and one round went into the hood. That one hit the engine and killed it.

The driver was a sheik and he was fit to be tied. He came totally unglued and starting pointing at everyone and going off. I tried to warn him. And I didn't feel sorry about it. His fault for trying to run the checkpoint. It don't really matter if he was a sheik and had a brand-new Mercedes. Rules is rules.

Rule number one: Don't kill women or children. Lots of things happen in war. We got mortared nightly and that can get pretty stressful. You're sleeping in the bunkers and you can't really do anything but sit and listen to the sounds. One time an RPG [rocket-propelled grenade] flew so close to my head that it melted the tape on my helmet. The only reason it didn't hit me full on in the chest was because I bent down to listen to what my sergeant was screaming at me. If I hadn't bent down, right smack-dab in the middle of my chest. Instead it just melted the tape on my helmet.

Another time, three mortars landed about forty meters away from where I was standing and the shrapnel ripped up my flak jacket's outer cover. I wasn't hit, but it's still pretty stressful when it's that close.

In Tikrit I was with the Special Forces unit. We worked with a lot of Iraqis, asking questions and finding out the lay of the land. This was back in 2003, just after the war started. We had been there for about a month and a half and were working with certain individuals to get information about people in the community that might be helpful for raids and stuff.

Information in war is useful. We had quite a few folks that would talk to us. There was one man in particular that gave us information. He had a daughter that was around eleven years old. The kids used to come up to the gate and play around us. Nothing very interesting, but it was nice to see kids around playing games. There was one boy named Ali who would give us information about who was in the Ba'th Party in the village and which house to check out.

I had these ranger beads that I used to count distances, and one day I couldn't find them. They were useful when you were in the field. Mine weren't army issued. They were beads that I had from fooling around in the woods, hunting and stuff. So I couldn't get replacement beads from my commander. Instead, I saw a girl and wondered whether she could tell me where to find some in the village. She was standing right there playing with her friends at the gate, so I decided to ask her.

"Hey, do you know somewhere around here that sells beads?" I asked her. She was standing by the gate that day, talking to two of her friends, and seemed open to talking with me.

"Beads?" she asked.

I tried to explain to her what the beads looked like. It might be a difficult thing to explain unless you have seen a picture of them. Ranger beads are a strand of beads, and the beads come in two sections. One section holds nine beads and the other section holds four beads. When you are counting paces, you transfer the nine beads first, and this corresponds with one transfer of the four beads. It's difficult to explain, and I don't think she understood what I was saying. So I was completely surprised when she came up to me one day with a strand of beads.

Now, ranger beads are typically brown or green and they are not very flashy, but the beads she got for me to replace my beads were brightly colored. Also, instead of two strands of nine and four beads, there was one strand of thirty bright beads. Purple, blue, yellow beads. Really, they weren't ranger beads at all. But it was real sweet of her to give them to me.

Two days after she got me the ranger beads, I saw her walking up to me at a checkpoint security. She was wearing a burqa and was all covered up. I didn't pick up on that at first, but I should have. She reached into her burqa when she got pretty close to me and pulled out a grenade. Threw it right at me. The grenade bounced off my gun and hit the Humvee that was sitting there. It bounced off the hood and blew up the tire. This is all about two feet away from where I was standing. The sergeant who was standing there with me had ducked behind the Humvee. The girl turned around and ran toward the gate.

I knew I couldn't let her reach the gate because there were too many people at the gate. For this same reason, I couldn't use my Mark Nineteen or 249 [a light machine gun] to shoot at her, so I had to use my nine millimeter. As I was watching her run toward the gate, I pulled out my gun and fired a warning shot toward her. She didn't even flinch.

The second shot hit her right shoulder. She stumbled a little, but she kept moving toward the gate. The next shot hit her left hip. She landed on the ground from that one but tried to get right back up.

I wasn't trying not to kill her. But she wouldn't stop moving toward the gate. So I shot her in the back of the leg. That put her on the ground.

The sergeant started running toward her, and I started running toward her. She had a cell phone in her hand, and he got to it first and kicked it out of her hand and away from her reach. He pulled the burqa back and she had C-four [a plastic explosive] strapped to a belt around her waist. The cell phone was wired. All she had to do was hit send on the cell phone.

I was trying to stop the bleeding, but she was bleeding out of the back and front of her left leg and also from her shoulder. Her eyes were open, but she didn't talk. She didn't look at me and didn't seem to be looking directly at anything. I could tell that she was having a lot of blood loss, so we were telling each other that we needed to get her an IV. We were trying to find the right bandage to use. I told the sergeant to leave me his bandages so he could find some more.

We had to stop the bleeding. But we couldn't. She died of blood loss. I had to shoot her. And I held her while she died.

The very next day I almost broke rule number two (Treat your enemy with respect). I didn't break the rule, but it's only on account of the fact that the enemy wasn't home. Had he been home, I'd have broken my rule.

We had to raid the girl's home. We checked with a couple of children from the neighborhood. No one knew that her father was part of the Ba'th Party. He wasn't very active in general and just seemed like an older guy. He was fairly old and injured. But on this day I was going after him.

We should have known something was different about him just from his house. In many of the neighborhoods over there, they put stucco walls up for fence lines. Stucco begins to crack over time because it is literally a big wall of mud. The stucco in front of his house didn't have as many cracks in it as his neighbors'. Turns out that he had some masonry stones in there that were covered over in stucco. He was hiding something and let us know all along. But we weren't looking in the right direction.

You have to understand a couple of things about raids. Raids are all about timing. By timing, I mean that raids happen quickly. You only have a certain amount of time to break through someone's house and grab what you need before they try and escape out the back door.

This means that during raids, everyone's adrenaline is pretty much pumping. My adrenaline was definitely pumping because I wanted this guy. I was so mad at him for using his daughter in that way. I don't blame her at all. It wasn't her fault that her father had instilled her determination with fanaticism. I don't think it was a personal thing from her at all. She was brainwashed by her father and doing what he wanted her to do. And it wasn't fair.

Our squad leader went to putting his shoulder into the gate in front and tried to kick through the bar, but the bar was not moving. We were trying to be quiet so he couldn't get through some back way, but in reality we were probably screaming and grunting like all get-out. We couldn't get the door open. So I took about six or seven steps back to get a running start and put my shoulder through the door. We got in.

My shoulder screamed with pain, and my right knee collapsed from the pressure I put on it to push through the door. All I cared about was getting into that house and getting ahold of that guy. But the pain going through my shoulder and knee wasn't allowing me to move anymore. My squad leader told me to stay right by the door as a rear security measure. He motioned for me to hold on to the shotgun. And I planned on using it.

The girl's father wasn't in the house. The only thing we were able to find was an Iraqi Air Force uniform and a bayonet. He got away.

I didn't sleep at all that night. Lay there and thought about what I would have done had he been in there. I'm ashamed to say that I would have made something up to have at him. It ate away at me that he wasn't in there. If I had gotten through the door sooner, would we have gotten him? There were several things that I wondered about.

I lay on my bed in the barracks and didn't close my eyes all night. My knee was screaming at me, but my thoughts were focused on him.

I wondered how much of that day he had seen. Did he sit somewhere so that he could have a view of the situation? Did he sit somewhere else on a cell phone talking to someone else with a view of the situation? I pictured him pacing with eyes intent, silently cheering for her to continue running toward the gate even though she was being shot. Was the cell phone in her hands wired to another cell phone in his hands? I wondered what he felt when he saw or heard about her stumbles. I wondered whether he watched me run toward her with my nine millimeter pointing toward her. I wondered what thoughts were going through his head when he saw the sergeant and me kneel down next to her. Whether he was concerned when we ran our hands over her body assessing for entry and exit wounds from the bullets. Whether he could see or feel the blood pouring out of her body like we did. Whether he could hear our tone when we discussed the need for an IV and bandages. Whether he silently raged for her to just die, right there in my hands.

He knew she would die that day, but did he know she would die like that? Was there any recognition that the mission was pointless for having involved his young daughter? Was any death worth it to him?

I have to say, I took it personally. Not from the girl. From him.

Symptoms: **Starving for Mercy**

Many individuals who suffer from emotional pain associated with a traumatic event experienced in war also have physical injuries. For some, it is difficult to focus away from the physical pain, particularly if the pain is chronic.

During his time in basic training, Hershel injured his knee to the extent that he had total reconstructive surgery performed. His time in basic training was extended for several months so that he had time to heal and strengthen the knee with physical therapy. During the raid on the girl's father's house in Iraq, Hershel reports that his knee collapsed as a result of the force with which he hit the steel door. Medics associated with his unit prescribed pain medication and physical therapy to treat and heal his reinjured knee and shoulder in theater ("in theater" means during his time in the war zone).

These injuries coincided with another injury sustained during his time in Iraq. He and three other soldiers lifted a trailer at the camp. A shot from a gun was fired, and the three other soldiers dropped the trailer in order to duck and cover. Hershel did not drop the trailer. He suffered a ruptured disk in his back.

Hershel reports that his physical suffering from the knee and back injuries was restrictive enough to limit his mobility, as well as his quality of life. Due to his pain, he began the process of separating from the army. His time in the army lasted for over four years. His discussions regarding that separation are not extensive.

In the seven years since his return from war, Hershel's quality of life has not improved. He continues to struggle with chronic pain associated with back and knee injuries. This results in irritability, agitation, and extreme frustration interpersonally. He receives pain medication from civilian doctors to manage the chronic pain.

Taking narcotic medication to treat chronic pain has long been associated with the risk of addiction. For a person to be considered addicted to a narcotic substance, two conditions are required. One condition is withdrawal, which is defined as the discomfort experienced when the substance is not taken. Withdrawal can be mild, in the form of physical and emotional discomfort, or severe and sometimes fatal. The second condition required for a person to be considered addicted to or dependent on a substance is tolerance. Tolerance is the state of needing higher doses of the substance to get the same effect. Therefore, to determine whether Hershel is addicted to the narcotic medications with which he treats his chronic pain, we would need to know whether he developed tolerance or experienced withdrawal.

Hershel reports that he ingests high doses of his narcotic medication in order to have any effect. He is currently taking three times the recommended dose. He reports that only certain physicians are comfortable prescribing this quantity of the medication for him. He prefers treatment from these physicians. He does not admit to experiencing withdrawal. Hershel indicates that what happens when he does not take his medication is that he experiences extensive physical pain. And that he becomes extremely irritable.

Many individuals who suffer from chronic pain experience relief initially through the use of medications. This relief is critical to their being able to tolerate the pain and function in their lives. Unfortunately, the relief gained through the use of narcotic substances is sometimes short-lived. This results in the individual using more of the medicine to get that same relief. And sometimes, a vicious circle begins.

Aside from chronic pain, Hershel also experiences difficulty in interpersonal relationships, has nightmares and flashbacks, and feels hopeless regarding the future. Chronic use of narcotic medications has long been associated with the increased likelihood of depression. Individuals with depression may have suicidal thinking. Hershel wishes for death daily.

Reexperiencing: Nightmares

Sleep can be a bit of a problem. Sometimes it is hard for me to go to sleep. I will wake up a bunch, or find it hard to breathe. Get cold sweats. Nightmares. I just feel anxious.

I have nightmares about that day. But the nightmares aren't really about that day so much as a theme about me stepping in front of someone who is about to get hurt. I'm always the one that gets shot or stabbed in my dream. Sometimes it's random, like I see someone that I haven't seen since high school walking through Walmart. Someone tries to stab him, so I jump in and take the wound myself.

One night I had a dream about a colleague at work. I do maintenance at a nonprofit apartment complex. There are 140 people that live in the complex, and they all are mentally ill or homeless. I know where everyone lives in the building, which resident lives in which apartment. Numbers are my thing.

I like most of the people I work with, you know, like the management. I try not to get any favorite residents. It's considered bad policy at work to interact with the residents much. We are there to fix maintenance problems. I work with one other guy. So, for example, if someone's stove isn't working, we get a call and are the ones to go out and determine what's wrong and fix it. I'm not allowed to work on appliances. I could do it, but I don't have my certificate. I could get my certificate, but management doesn't want to pay for me to do that. It doesn't make sense because that would make the system work better, but I have no say-so.

In my dream one night, I am standing in the office. I need to grab some tools but stop for a minute to get a drink of water from the water cooler in the office. In the office, two girls are sitting at their desks talking to each other. They are talking about getting lunch together, and plan for one girl to go and grab the food and bring it back so that they can eat together. I remember that part because they are planning on eating at Taco Xpress. I like their tacos and am thinking it sounds good.

The next thing that happens is that shots fire and the girls start screaming. One girl screams while sitting there at her desk. The other girl disappears somewhere. She might have ducked under her desk or disappeared somewhere into thin air. Nightmares are strange like that.

Well, the girl sitting at her desk screaming is just sitting there being a target. I can see someone moving outside the front window of the office. This guy is dressed in black and I can't see him all that good but can tell that he is the one firing. He starts looking in the window right at that girl sitting at her desk screaming. She is looking right back at him too. I can see him point his nine millimeter right at her through the window, and that's when I start moving toward her. I dive. I know that I need to be between her and the bullet. I hear the gunfire while I am in the air.

And suddenly it's quiet. She's not screaming anymore. There's an echo from the gunfire, but other than that it is quiet. I feel the bullet enter my abdomen. It feels like fire. I land on top of her desk. The first thing I need to know is that she is OK. I look at her and she is looking at my stomach. She is crying. The guy outside with the gun disappears. He is done with his job. And I know I am not going to live. And I wake up.

Another nightmare involved my cousin being locked up in a cage. I don't even know why I would think of that or why he was being held captive. I had to sneak over to him and open up the cage to pull him out. When I get him out, someone starts shooting at him to kill him. I step in front of that bullet and get shot myself. I can't talk about how graphic it got then, but let's just say that I end up killing the guy in a knife fight. I'm always the one that is getting hurt.

Reexperiencing: Beads

I don't like to think about that day in Iraq by the guard's tower. It's easier for me not to think about it. I have that little girl's beads that she gave me, though. I keep them with me so that I won't forget her. I have them in my bedroom right by the lamp next to my bed. I keep them there. As a memory.

I talk to them a bit. They help me remember her. I had to kill her to save the people at the gate from getting blown up. But it kills me that she had no bearing on what was right or wrong. She believed what her father told her. She lost so much blood.

I could kick myself in the ass for not shooting her in the leg first. I had the time to fire four rounds. That means I had time to think about the situation for a second. We are trained to hit center mass, and the biggest target on her would have been her back. But I knew that I wanted to stop her and not kill her. So I aimed around her back a little bit. I should've thought about hitting her in the leg first, instead of that last shot.

It's hard to think in that situation, though. You've only got seconds to assess and act. When I look at the beads, I always think about that day. I am an emotion-driven person. I have to remind myself to step back, look at the situation before making a decision. It's just hard

to hold down those emotions. The beads sit there for me every day.
A reminder.

Avoidance

I am *done*. I am *done*. I don't want to do this anymore. I don't want
to be here.

I woke up again this morning. You'd think I'd just die in my
sleep. Nothing worth living for anyway. Everything is all messed up.
Always been messed up and it always will be messed up. I don't even
want to start the day off.

All I want to do is go off by myself and live in the woods. Then I
wouldn't have to deal with people, at least. Damn stupid people. No
one listens to me. I can't seem to communicate with my roommates
or work or friends or girlfriends.

Every time I get a girlfriend, it goes south. I don't understand
what happens. I try my damnedest to make situations better. I work
hard, and everything fails horribly. And I know that doing the same
thing over and over again and expecting different results is the defini-
tion of insanity, but nothing ever seems to go right.

I wouldn't actually do anything to hurt myself, even though I think
about dying every day. I don't want to live. But I'm not going to take
the coward's way out (rule number three). Maybe it's an army thing,
but I'm not going to do anything to intentionally hurt myself. But I
wouldn't stop anyone else if they wanted to shoot me. If someone
were standing right in front of me with a gun pointed right at me, I
would be happy. I might even do something to provoke him to make
sure he'd go ahead and do it. But I wouldn't intentionally hurt myself.

I don't have any friends. I don't have a girlfriend. The situation
with my roommates is getting worse and worse. Helps when I have
someone to talk to, but it seems hard.

Here's an example of the type of stuff that happens with one of my
roommates. One random Monday I bought a bag of candy. You know,
those bags that have about forty individually wrapped candy bars

in them? I felt like having some candy and thought my roommates might like some too, so I put the bag in a cabinet that we all use. Stuff in there means that everyone can have some.

I was having a bit of trouble sleeping that night so I went down to the kitchen for a piece of candy. And I couldn't believe it. There were only about five or six left. I stood there for a minute. Kinda fuming. I mean, I bought the candy for everyone to have some, but I kinda expected it to take a little longer than a couple of hours before they were almost all gone. And I bought the damn bag and there were only a [few] left. So I decided to take the rest of them back to bed with me. At least I had a couple of pieces of candy, since I wasn't sleeping anyway.

About half an hour went by before my roommate stuck his head in the door and said, "Hey, asshole! Why'd you eat all the candy?"

"I didn't eat all the candy! There were only about five or six pieces left when I got to them." I was kinda fuming before, but now I was feeling pissed off.

He said, "There were twenty pieces of that candy left. Why'd you go and eat them all?"

"There were not twenty pieces of candy left. There were five or six."

"No, there weren't. There were like twenty pieces. You're always going off and taking everything. Why'd you even share with us in the first place if you were going to go off and eat all of them anyway?"

"There were five or six pieces." Now I was starting to have to stand up outta my bed and I was getting all agitated because he wouldn't listen to me. And I knew he was the one that ate all the candy in the first place and here he was accusing me of eating all the candy, when I was the one that bought the candy and hardly got any of it.

I grabbed the wrappers that were sitting on my desk next to my bed and started to smooth them out. He was still standing at my door looking at me like I owed him some candy, or like maybe I got some more hidden away in my room and if he just stood there long enough, I'd pass it over to him. Only thing is, I ain't got no more candy in my room because I shared what I had with him.

So I started smoothing out the candy wrappers and counting for him to see that I didn't eat twenty pieces. "One . . . two . . . three . . . four . . . five . . . six. See, there were six pieces of candy. That's all I had. You were the one that ate the rest."

"That's bullshit," he replied. "Just because you have six wrappers sitting there next to your bed doesn't mean you didn't eat all the candy. I know you did and it's not even fair. I mean, why share with us in the first place?"

I got up and slammed my door shut. I couldn't take talking to him no more. I could hear him mumbling down the hall, but I didn't care to hear what he had to say. It's like he needs some sort of convincing all the time, but you can never convince him of nothing. He's too used to being disagreeable. Like he's irritated about something and everyone around him always has to pay for it even though we didn't get him irritated in the first place. You can hear him and his girlfriend fighting until like five or six in the morning. He still acts the same as he did when we were thirteen years old. He's irritable and controlling. He's not fun to live with. And then I really couldn't get back to sleep.

I remember this one other time he accused me of stealing his Pop-Tarts. I didn't even know he had Pop-Tarts. I don't even *like* Pop-Tarts! But just like this time, we started arguing and there was nothing I could say to convince him that I didn't steal his damn Pop-Tarts. I feel like with him, I only matter when he wants something.

I have the same trouble with girls. Like this one girl in particular. We were getting along pretty good for a while and then we stopped talking. I don't know what happened, but she stopped answering my e-mails. So we didn't talk for about three weeks and then all of a sudden she pops up and asks what the deal is. She said that it seemed like I wanted her to stop calling.

I didn't want her to stop calling, though. She stopped answering me. I just don't even know what happens, but everything in my life goes south. So what I would really like to do is pack up a couple of bags and go live under a bridge.

Hyperarousal

I smoke three packs of cigarettes a day. I am agitated. Maybe those cigarettes aren't really helping me, but hell, I am agitated. I don't sleep. I'm in constant pain. I got two injuries from my time in basic and in Iraq. My knee and my back. To deal with the pain, I gotta take pain medicines. If I don't take enough, they don't get rid of the pain. If I take enough to get rid of the pain, I overmedicate.

Everything and everybody gets on my nerves. What I'd like to do is get one of those nonfunctional machine guns and mount it to the back of my window in my truck. I'd put orange paint on the barrel so that people know it's not loaded. My message would be to "drive friendly." I just don't understand people.

It's common courtesy. You only have to move your finger one tiny little inch to hit the turn signal. Come on. You've got two thousand pounds of steel and you're going really fast. It's just common courtesy to tell people where you're going.

Reminds me of something that happened once in Iraq after I killed that little girl. I was on a convoy mission doing rear security. There were about seventy-five fuel tankers on the side of the road. I was on top of the vehicle getting antsy because this other vehicle was coming up on us going about sixty miles per hour. I had the Mark Nineteen [big grenade launcher], but I couldn't use that weapon against this vehicle because it was getting too close. Grenades have to turn a certain number of times before they explode, so you need to be a certain distance away from the target to use the Mark Nineteen. The 249 SAW [squad automatic weapon] is a little more precise, so I picked up that weapon and started screaming at this vehicle to stop.

In Arabic, the word for stop is *akeif.* And I was screaming it at the top of my lungs. I didn't see anything else. I didn't feel anything but this complete focus and rage against this vehicle coming up on us so fast. I wanted to kill the person driving this vehicle. The vehicle just kept coming closer and closer to us. I was screaming for them to stop, but I had my weapon up and ready to fire. I needed this guy to come just a little closer. I knew David (another member of my squad) was standing outside our Humvee also screaming for the car to stop. When the vehicle finally did stop, all this dust was kicked up into the air. David was hit. I didn't see him, but I knew he had just been hit by this vehicle, and I was going to kill the driver.

I pointed my weapon right at him and pulled the trigger. Nothing happened. The first round was a dud. So I picked up my nine millimeter and fired three rounds into the vehicle.

I heard this guy screaming, "I'm sorry. I'm sorry. I am drunk. I can't drive. I am drunk."

David rolled out from under our Humvee. I thought he was dead, but now he was looking at me and yelling for me to stop. I had somehow jumped out of the top of the Humvee, and I was getting ready to tackle this guy. "I should've killed you!" I screamed. "I should've killed you!"

It was everything I could do to hold myself back. David was right there holding my arms and trying to make eye contact with me, but I couldn't take my eyes off this Iraqi guy. This guy who was drunk and almost killed my friend. I held myself back that day. But I really wanted to kill him.

Recovery: **Moving Forward**

If you're going through hell, keep going.

—Winston Churchill

Every day is a constant battle, and I would say that some days I hide it better than others. I think back on that day a lot. I try and stay in touch with some of the guys that were in my squad. Certain memories make me laugh.

I remember this one time we were putting sandbags around the turret. We needed as much protection as we could get up there. Shots were firing and we were anxious. Almost frantically piling up sandbags.

I said, "Gimme one of your cigarettes."

My friend stopped piling for a minute and looked at me holding his sandbag. He said, "You don't smoke."

I said, "I do now."

That's how things were over there, and I'm not sure life has calmed down much for me back home. I'm not getting fired at all the time, but I carry the weight of the lessons with me. And I still smoke. Some days more than others.

I have some plans. I have decided to leave the state that I've been living in for more than the last eight years. It's time to go home. There is a school there that has a good program of study for me. I would like to train to become a game warden. Also, the VA there is good. I used to go there with my grandfather. He was a cranky old fellow, but they treated him real good. The VA where I'm at now isn't so friendly.

I think the only thing that kept me going for the last eight years is spite. People get ideas in their heads about me and what I'm going to do, and I'm not going to let them be right.

Like the physician at the VA that was supposed to be treating a calcium deposit in the tear duct in my eye. Seems like a simple thing for her to take care of, but she assumed that I was some kind of drug addict or something and started going off about me taking a drug test. Said that she wasn't going to treat me until I got a urinalysis.

I have to admit that I don't look good. My hair is long and I have several piercings. Plus, I was nodding off a little during our meeting, but that's on account of the medicine that was prescribed to me. I did what she asked of me and things ended up working out OK. She was much nicer after she received the results of the urinalysis.

It's time for me to look forward. I'm moving back to my home. My choice is to help my mom out a little with things for her home. I'm going to put new shingles on the house and fix her air-conditioning. Take care of things that she can't.

And then I'm going to find a place for myself. I think in five years,

I will work in one of the national parks, and I'll be able to do what I actually want to do. I've been taking care of other people for a long time, and it's taken its toll on my body. It's time for me to be on my own path for a while.

Today I am breathing easier and have hope. I don't have to fight my own self anymore. I have this recurring dream where I fight my shadow. No matter what I do to the shadow, nothing fazes it. I could fire a weapon, load another clip, fire again, load another clip, and fire again. Nothing happens. I can't kill him. I could crack him in the teeth and he just laughs.

I think I'm realizing that I've been fighting my nature. I hold my emotions back, but I don't need to. I'm strong enough to keep fighting.

I think in all of us there is a tendency to want the happy ending. We all want to know that things turn out in the end. Chicago Cubs fans throughout the world can relate to this sentiment. Even though that baseball team hasn't won a World Series since 1908, true Cubs fans start each new year with hope.

And it's this type of hope that Hershel's story offers us. His ideals were tested during his deployment to war, and his ability to work through the physical and emotional pain serves to remind all of us about that great concept of "hope."

Although I would love to see the day when the Cubs win the series, I have complete faith that people like Hershel make this world a much better place. Just because they are in it.

CHAPTER 3

The Storm before the Calm: Alex's Story

BEFORE TRAUMA: **The Misfit**

ALEX'S STORY WAS DIFFICULT TO CHRONICLE. I found myself wanting to change it, to protect the truth from being known. It was tempting to alter aspects of Alex's unpleasant reality. I felt a responsibility for the written words. And I felt a responsibility for Alex. In the end, I knew this was not my decision to make. It was my responsibility to hear the story. And to tell it. And it was painful.

When I think of the concept of resilience, I like to think about what happens in nature each spring. Each winter in the Northeast, trees are stripped bare. Animals fatten up. Chipmunks' coats turn red, and birds that do not fly south for the winter begin to resemble butterballs. The earth takes on a brownish color. Skies turn dark way too early. People wish for naps and prefer to eat warm and heavy foods. All you see of people are their chunky coats and clunky boots. Snowstorms appear. Winter is heavy.

But no matter how storm-ridden and cold the winter is, spring will arrive. Leaves will begin to bud. Green will slowly start to reappear. Energy feels renewed. You haven't heard a bird chirp in months, and yet there it is. You hear one! You might think, "I did it! I survived another cold winter."

Admittedly, many individuals in the Northeast prefer winter. These people do not cry or tear up in relief when green little buds emerge on trees and shrubs. They do not have thoughts of salvation. There are people who grieve the cold white snow when it begins to melt.

Yet, if you are one of those people who light up at the coming of spring, you might understand a thing or two about Alex. Alex is like the turning of winter into spring. He has energy and light. His words are short and fast. His wit is quick. Just like that barren field in winter, you get the sense that given enough time and warmth, he will bounce back, amazingly unharmed.

My guess is that those who have tried to hold back Alex's energy found him impossible. Exasperating, even. With all that energy, why all the darkness? Then I remember: it is only because of the darkness that we appreciate the light.

My parents adopted me when I was three days old, and my hyperactivity did not impress them. I have a theory on what went wrong: children should be raised by their natural parents. It's too hard for some people to relate to other people that are too different from them.

I don't think my adopted parents ever understood me. I'm not complaining or saying they didn't try or that there was something wrong with them. I'm just saying that it's possible that my natural mother and father would've understood where I was coming from better, and been able to handle me better. As it was, the fact that I was hyperactive was not appreciated or dealt with very well.

They thought something was seriously wrong with me. And more importantly, they thought they could somehow fix it. They spent years trying to figure it out, and I think all that figuring led to things just getting worse. I don't think anything was wrong with me. I just think I engaged in more than my fair share of normal acting up.

Then again, they were working so hard to get me to be different, maybe I was retaliating somehow. The more they tried to get me to change and calm down, the worse things got. I couldn't be them. I was me.

When I was six years old, my adopted parents got divorced and my mom moved several states away. She took me with her. It was kind of a bad setup because she was perfect and I was hyper. I had a hard time in school because I had a terrible attention span. She took me to all kinds of doctors and therapists to make me start acting more like her. That was fine, except I think I had too much of it. I was put on all kinds of medications for ADHD [attention-deficit/hyperactivity disorder] and depression before I was even ten years old. Another parent may not have made such a big deal of things.

When you have a lot of therapy as a child, you learn to talk to adults in a different way. You can talk to adults about all kinds of things, but you can also learn pretty quickly how to get a rise out of people. Sometimes, I would get angry at all the attention and start to suggest that things were worse than they were.

I don't know why I did that. It never made anything better. In fact, things always got worse when I would say things like that. But I think I was getting fed up with the whole thing. They were going to accuse me of stuff anyway.

When I was nine, my mother remarried. She married a complete jerk. I did not like him. And, no surprise, he did not like me either. I would say that my stepfather and I had major issues. It was so bad that they put me in a hospital for a couple of weeks. Once when I was ten and once when I was twelve.

When I was thirteen, my adopted mother adopted a baby with my stepfather. And again, it should be no surprise that this poor kid is now having the same issues I used to have. He is a smart kid but has a lot of issues. He's being sent to therapy and put on medications because he is not acting right. Don't people ever wonder? She was two for two in terms of having children with problems. Why would both of her children magically have all this need for counseling and medications?

It's possible that some people should not have children and that's why God doesn't give them the biological means to have children of their own. They shouldn't go against God's will. They should work on accepting that reality rather than adopting other people's children. I don't know if that is true, but it seems true with my case.

After my mother adopted another baby, I acted out with matches. That got me sent to live with my father. What kids aren't interested in matches at some point in their lives? Matches are cool. They can set things on fire. I didn't hurt anybody. I just played with matches.

After I moved back to my adopted father's house, I got really interested in spy tactics and weapons. Because I had that as an interest, my parents were always concerned that I was thinking of hurting myself. I wasn't. But they were always asking why I wanted to learn more about guns and stuff. Parents.

I really messed up one day, though. My dad told me that it was time to go to my therapy session. I wasn't in the mood to go that day. I was in my room messing with my stuff. See, I loved anything to do with weapons and spy tactics. Over the years, I had become excellent with a rubber band. Rubber bands make outstanding slingshots. I had learned to sling M-Eighties [large firecrackers]. This did not go over well with my parents, but they liked it even less when I took an interest in making explosives and did quite a bit of pyrotechnics. I also became an expert at picking locks. I was able to get into places that no one else could. I would run around in a ninja suit in the daytime trying not to be seen.

On this particular day, I was messing with some M-Eighties to see what kind of damage they could do. My dad knocked on my door and said, "Come on, Alex. It's time to go to therapy." Sigh.

"Dad, I don't feel like going today," I said. "Can I skip it?"

"No. Let's go. What are you doing in there?"

"I'm just messing with my stuff."

He opened the door and looked in, and it was a mess. I was working with some fireworks to see what I could add to them to see if they could be even more lethal. Like thumbtacks. Stuff was all over the room, but I think it was the smell that bothered him. I had lit the fuse a couple of times.

He stood there looking in my door with a look on his face that I knew meant he was angry. And I was feeling defensive. I couldn't ever have any fun.

"I'll clean it up, Dad. I was just messing around."

"Let's go," he said. The tone in his voice was not friendly.

Instead of cleaning it up, I just sighed. I looked down at the mess and felt some satisfaction. At least I learned that thumbtacks could be lethal.

You would think that I would have just stopped myself there, but I went and made things even worse when I got to the session that day. I told my psychiatrist that I was playing with explosives because I wanted to hurt myself. I wonder now if I just figured that they were going to believe whatever they were going to believe anyway, so I might as well go along. Big problem with that plan. They sent me to a psych unit.

Had I known that they were going to institutionalize me ("for your own good") that day, I wouldn't have said what I said. I just said it so they would leave me alone.

When I got out of the hospital, I was so upset with my dad that I told him I was smoking crack. At this point, he was done with me. He put me in a group home. Some seriously bad kids live in group homes. And I learned a lot about some seriously bad things while I lived there. I wasn't doing very well in school and was put in an alternative school. The neighborhood was bad. It was all bad. So I decided to go back to live with my mom.

Guess what happened at my mom's house? Things did not improve. I was not wanted. There were all kinds of rules, like crazy rules about not being able to be in the house alone and not being able to have a key to my home. I always had to find something to do until they came home from work. They were Jewish and extremely religious, and I did not fit into their world. It was frowned upon whenever I would not eat kosher. She wanted to enforce a lot of control over me. I wasn't able to experiment or figure things out for myself. I could never have electronic games or things. Even if I did have something, there were all sorts of hoops I would have to jump through just to be able to interact with the toy for a twenty-minute stretch of time. By the time I was fourteen or fifteen years old, I had been to so much therapy and talked to so many crazy people that I felt like I was just getting set up for failure.

But I knew I believed in myself. I believe in people and I like to do good. But I did not have a family environment that told me I was good. And I was not good at school. This posed problems. I didn't have direction or support. My dad used to tell me I would be eighteen before I knew it. Love is awkward.

So, it is probably no surprise that I started to hang out with the wrong crowd during all that time I was locked out of the house. I began to experiment with alcohol and drugs. One day at school, I got frustrated with a teacher and walked away saying, "Fuck you. I hope you like the bomb." I must be an extremely slow learner, because every time I made statements like this, my life would only get worse. And guess what? I was expelled from school. My new school was a level six boys' home for juvenile delinquents.

I wish I could say things started to get better for me during this time in my life, but things got a little worse before they started to get better. It's hard to get better when you are so frustrated and no one believes in you. I believed in myself, but I couldn't figure out how to get where I wanted to go. So for a while longer, I continued to be a part of my own problem.

I was so frustrated and disgusted living at a level six boys' home. The kids that live at those places are crazy. I learned all sorts of things about drugs. It was all a mess. I started to think in my head that maybe if I could hang out at the beach for a couple of days, I could clear my head and figure out how to get where I wanted to be.

If you don't know anything about level six boys' homes, you can't just head over to the beach to walk around and clear your head. It was a good plan, though. It makes sense that I would need someplace to walk around and that I would need to clear my head. You could even say that the fact that I was aware my head was totally off balance was a really good sign. The fact that I knew I needed to clear my head so that I could get on a path and make good decisions was a great sign. But in reality, I couldn't get to the beach. I couldn't just ask someone if I could go hang out at the beach for a couple of days to clear my head. I didn't know who to ask, and even if I did know who to ask, [that person was] not going to give me permission. [The people at the home] didn't particularly care that I needed a couple of days off. They didn't want to deal with me at all.

In my mind, I could hear the waves crashing down. I could feel the warm sun touching my skin, the sand underneath my shoes, and the breeze taking things away. I didn't really picture other people around, just the idea of being able to think for a minute or two about the situation I was in. To look out at the water and know there was a big world out there. To know that not all life was inside that group home. That time would move forward, and that I could move in the direction I wanted to go, if only I could figure out what steps to take to get there. I felt like I could breathe at the beach, and that I needed to get there as soon as possible. Some of my stress could be taken care of if I could just get there. The beach was only about an hour away.

So I decided I had to take the situation into my own hands. I had to figure out how to break out of that place and steal a car. I knew how to get a car. My new friends at the group home taught me all about grand theft auto. It's not that complicated. So I really just needed an opportunity to break away.

When the opportunity came, I took it. Stole a car and drove straight toward the water. The beach was pretty cool. It was almost like I thought it would be. There was sun, sand, water, and a breeze. But there were also a lot of people. I didn't think about all the people, yet they made it easy to find food. Harder to find my sense of peace, though. There was actually quite a bit going on at the beach. But I got picked up by the authorities after only a week there. They sent me back and put me in a maximum-security home.

I know it's hard to believe, but things started to get better for me for a while. When I turned eighteen, I moved back up north by my dad and met my biological mother for the first time. Turns out that I also had a brother. He found me, and it was really a great thing he did.

My brother has got his shit together. He has a family and a good job and has all his p's and q's. Man, it's great to have a brother. My biological mother has some issues, though. You only have to be around her for about twenty seconds before you realize that she has a serious mental illness. My mother has schizophrenia, and that was why she gave me up for adoption.

After meeting my biological relatives, it was easier for me to put together my plan. I hadn't graduated from high school yet because I was way too busy acting up. So I started by getting my GED and planning for my life. And I knew what life I wanted. I wanted to be a soldier. I loved the idea of a soldier's life. Soldiers don't go around acting up like I was, so I needed to get myself together.

I know it sounds amazing, but I did OK. Between the ages of eighteen and twenty-four, I had my shit together. I got my GED and worked at several jobs. I had a daughter and got married.

All right, I will admit that I had one slip during that time. And it was totally stupid, but I was desperate. My baby needed diapers and I didn't have enough money that week. So I went to Walmart and stole a pack of diapers and baby formula. They caught me on video. So I had a misdemeanor retail theft added to my list of problems with the law.

At twenty-four years old, I joined the National Guard. In the Guard, I could stay at home for my daughter to work but could also experience soldier life. In the Guard, you typically have to work one weekend a month and serve for two weeks in the summer. We were a country at war and I knew the Guard was being sent to serve in this war, so I figured I would be deployed at some point. And I was.

Trauma: **Iraq**

Life in Iraq was OK. One of my jobs over there was to escort suspected terrorists from one zone to another so that they were always in movement and harder for other terrorists to track down and kill. That kind of job can make a person anxious. But it was OK.

I also worked with Iraqi Correctional Officers. That was a cool job because you could teach. I was good at that. We had one stressful day where we had to get 120 of them on base and maintain control. We got them safely there.

Nothing bad really happened to me off base. Bad things only happened on base.

The worse thing happened at Camp Liberty in Baghdad. Camp Liberty is the biggest base over in Iraq. It's like a small town. It used to be one of Saddam's palaces and is located close to the Baghdad airport. The palace has reflecting lights around it, with big domes and turrets. Turquoise is placed around the castle to offset the sand-colored stucco walls of the castle. T-walls are all over the place, like they are set up around the dining facility and the gym in case of a car bomb or mortar attack. The compound itself can hold well over ten thousand troops, has a gym, a stress clinic, a PX (which stands for post exchange, meaning that you can purchase all sorts of items there, including a TV), and a food court. Security coming in and out of Camp Liberty is good, so when you are walking around the base, you feel safe. Nothing is going to explode right next to you.

But you are in Baghdad, so it is hot. It's at least a hundred degrees and is a big dust bowl. Dust covers the bushes because it is hot and doesn't rain often. You walk around in a constant state of sweatiness.

But even though it is hot and you are sweaty, you feel a little better walking around Camp Liberty because of the security. It really is like a small town. Soldiers are always in uniform, unless they are walking to the gym and then they are in their physical training gear. Soldiers always have their weapons on them, even if they are going to work out. It's regulation. You are even supposed to wear your weapon if you are going to the bathroom, but I'm not sure everyone does. Inside the compound, you would see uniformed soldiers walking to their jobs or to the dining facility or to the gym or to go and pick up their laundry. People are moving around. Vehicles are also in a state of constant movement inside the compound. Some are parked, but it seems like there are vehicles everywhere. It's crowded. And hot.

During the nighttime, lights from a generator light up the compound. This gives you a sense of the constant state of work going on inside. It is like a small town with a big-city military attitude.

So when you walk around the camp, you are surrounded by activity and motion. People walking around, vehicles driving around, and action. You are in a war zone, so you even get used to certain sounds, like gunfire and explosions. Inside the camp, you wouldn't necessarily expect to hear gunfire, but you are already fairly accustomed to that type of noise, so you might not even flinch.

On this day I was walking around the camp, and when I got close to the stress clinic I heard gunfire. The stress clinic is a place that people go to get help when they are struggling emotionally. Sometimes command makes people go over there and talk to the professionals. So, for example, if you are jumpy and causing fights and stuff, command might force you to go and talk to someone in the stress clinic. I'm not sure what could get a person sent to see a doctor, because every commander is different, but it is generally for people who seem to be struggling. You wouldn't necessarily know if someone was having really bad nightmares unless he was screaming out loud in the middle of his sleep and trying to punch people, but you would know if someone was having problems with anger and was causing problems with morale. Some commanders might just have a talk with the soldier, but others might send him in for some professional help. The stress clinic would be one of those places for help.

It can be a little hard to tell for each person what might help him. Sometimes a guy just needs to be around more positive people. You know, he's missing home or having trouble with his wife back at home or something, and he's in a bad mood because of that. Those guys just might need to be around other guys who can help keep them focused and make them laugh and stuff. You know, they might just need some perspective and support.

With other guys, it might work better if they were put in a situation that was pretty structured, where they felt they were being productive and kept busy. This could help them keep their minds off whatever is bothering them.

But with some guys, they need professional help. Like, if everything else fails, you know, like if they started to avoid hanging out with other dudes and they didn't care what command said to them and they were causing trouble during missions, then they might need to be called in for better help.

I don't know the answers, and I think every situation is different. Sometimes you just have to figure things out as you go.

So on this one day, I was walking by the stress clinic and heard gunfire. I looked up and saw a soldier in uniform running out of the clinic. He started firing his weapon, which was a thirty-round magazine. I watched as he started shooting at other soldiers in the area. I saw him shoot three soldiers in uniform and two wearing PT gear.

I ran back behind the T-wall barrier and took a minute to lock and load my Beretta. I had to get myself armed and ready because this guy was firing. If I hadn't run behind the T-wall, he could have easily looked in my direction and shot me too.

I stood back up to go around the T-wall and take him down, but by the time I did that I could see him on the ground being apprehended by a group of other soldiers.

Five soldiers were killed that day and three wounded. All by a fellow soldier. One of our own. At a stress clinic.

Man, that messed me up because you gotta be able to trust your own guys.

I knew right away what was happening. Being on guard saved my life. If he had just looked my way, he would have shot me too. That was the worst thing to deal with. Someone on our own side causing that kind of damage.

SYMPTOMS: **Child's Play**

I told the chain of command that it was not a good idea to let me go home. I asked if I could stay on active duty for a while longer. I didn't feel ready to go home and knew that I was going to struggle.

They said, "You'll be OK."

I was not OK.

That whole situation messed me up. Things didn't feel right. You have to trust your own men. And I do. But dude, this happened right in front of me, in a place where it shouldn't have happened, by one of our own. Things were not OK in my head about that situation.

Reexperiencing

I don't really remember my dreams, but I have flashbacks about that situation. Flashes when I'm awake, but in my mind I see that soldier killing other soldiers. I see it just like when I was there. I remember everything that happened, and flashes of it will pop up in my head. I always have a loaded weapon on me because of this.

It was the worse thing really, someone on our side doing damage to our own people. It's not right.

Avoidance

I didn't want to think when I first got home. I was on edge. To combat the stress that didn't make sense to me, I started drinking pretty heavily and smoking pot. I just didn't want to deal with things for a while. Nothing was going my way yet, and I was having a hard time finding a consistent job. I had some part-time work going from house to house trying to get people to sign up with a cell phone company. One day, another friend and I were out in this rich neighborhood trying to convince people to sign up, and we must have scared this one woman. When we got back to our car, she must have called the police on us and reported that we were in her neighborhood and on substances. The police came and we were still sitting there in the car, smoking weed.

So the police came up to the car and they could smell the weed and they said, "What's going on, fellas?"

I opened the car door and said, "We're just working a little bit today."

"Most people don't work and use drugs at the same time. Get out of the car."

My friend didn't say anything, but I knew we were totally caught and there was no use lying.

I said, "I'm sorry. I just got back from a tour in Iraq. I'm pissed off that I can't find a regular job. I'm angry about my living situation, and I'm using to try and take the edge off. I admit it. It was me."

The cop looked through the car and found our stuff. He also found my military badge and said, "You just got back?"

"Yes sir. I got back a couple of months ago. It's hard to find work right now."

He told me to come and sit with him in his car and he wrote a ticket out for possession. I didn't get a DUI because I wasn't driving the car when he drove up. My friend drove the car back home.

I got off easy that time. And I really wish I had learned my lesson at that point. But I didn't. Far from it.

That very night after I was back at home, I was pissed off that I had gotten a ticket. I had been doing so well for so long, and I could feel myself on that slippery slope. Just to prove to myself how slippery, I decided to get drunk that night. A friend of mine was using PCP, and I decided to try it. It's like a cigarette with PCP in it, and formaldehyde. I loved it.

It feels so good when you smoke it, and you don't worry at all anymore about not having a job and not being able to pay the bills. When you smoke it, you don't worry about anything. That felt great to me.

I was living with my dad at that point, and he could see the path I was on, so he told me I had to move out. Things were not going my way. So far, I had gotten a ticket, I was using drugs, I hadn't found a job yet, I had no money to find a new place, my unemployment hadn't kicked in yet, and I was out of a place to live. This was a bad day. And about to get worse.

I put everything I owned in my Chevy Tahoe. I probably had about ten thousand dollars' worth of possessions in that truck, including electronics and clothes and stuff. I was drunk and high on PCP. I was hanging out with the guys that introduced PCP to me earlier that day because, clearly, they were my new friends and totally trustworthy. So I followed them downtown. I can't actually remember what happened next, but I can tell you what I was told. The guys stole my truck and my possessions.

You might have seen that one coming, but hang on a second. Wait until you hear what I did. Apparently, I was walking along the street and came across a young girl and her uncle. I bumped into the young girl and threw her. I have no idea why I would have done that.

A note about PCP: PCP has been associated with hallucinations and memory loss. Individuals taking large doses of PCP are capable of becoming psychotic, aggressive, and violent.

I understand the uncle had a couple of friends in the immediate area and called for them to come over and help him protect the girl against me. Although I don't know how many people came over to help, they beat me up. I lost my glasses and I can't see without my glasses. I understand that even though I was out of my mind on drugs and couldn't see without my glasses, I fought back.

The police arrived and I spent the next three weeks in jail. I was charged with attempted kidnapping, although this charge was eliminated and reduced to assault on the guys that came to rescue the girl.

Two good things came out of that situation. My real brother came to help bail me out of jail, and I got my truck back. All of my possessions were gone, though.

You might think this would have been a good opportunity for a wake-up call. It was. But I didn't answer. Instead, I got all twisted in my head. I felt frustrated and sick. I knew my situation in Iraq was a good time for me to get to know my potential. I was a good soldier. People recognized my skills. It was the first time people said I was good at what I did. And it was true. I was good at what I did. I was a good soldier. I loved supporting my country and being good. And now I was back in the States and had nothing to show for it. I hated that I had saved up money in Iraq to make good choices and I had already squandered opportunities away.

And I was back in trouble with the law.

Why would I want to get messed up all the time again? It was foolish to use PCP again. But I did. I met up with a couple of girls passing out flyers on the street. Instead of talking to them, I should've turned away and gone home instead. My daughter was back at my house with my wife. My wife is not my daughter's mother, but she was taking care of her for me. I was only supposed to be gone for a short while. But the girls were friendly and fun and we started talking. One of them asked me if I smoked wet. I said yes. So they asked if I wanted to hang out with them. Turns out I did.

After a while I decided it was time to go home. On my drive back home, I pulled over on the side of the road to sit and smoke weed. As you can tell, I wasn't thinking too clearly. I jumped out of my car while it was still running, which scared a couple of bystanders. One of them called for the police to come because I had gone into the wooded area off the road. They told the police it looked like I was hunting in the weeds.

When the cops showed up, they weren't all that afraid of me and my hunting weapons, which turned out to be my fingers. I must've been hallucinating that I was back in Iraq and was playing soldier.

It wasn't funny, because then I was in jail and I needed to get my daughter back to her mother. I asked if I could call my wife. She was furious with me and threatened to leave me. She didn't want to take care of my daughter. Didn't seem concerned for her well-being. Was basically saying that she was done with the whole mess. I was begging for her to call my daughter's mother so that she could come and get her, but she didn't want to. So I begged the cop to call my daughter's mother so that she could come and get her. After a while, they took care of the situation.

I will never forget worrying about my daughter that night. I just wanted her to get back to her mother. And I had another possession charge on my record. I was in and out of jail in a couple of hours that time, although it felt much longer because of the drama with my wife and daughter. I can't say that my head was in a good space. I was still pissed off about how things were going in my life. I couldn't believe I was having drama with my wife. I couldn't believe that I had no money saved up and that I couldn't pay my rent that month. It was around the first of the month and the rent was due. It was also the time of the month that drill happened. I was feeling stressed.

Drill weekends start at eight o'clock on Saturday morning. Usually we do stuff until around five or six that night and then report back again on Sunday morning. Drill weekends only happen once a month, usually the first weekend of the month unless something unusual is going on.

So my head was not in the game on that particular Saturday morning. I was full of stinking thinking. I decided that what would help me reduce my stress would be to have a little more PCP in my system. 'Cause that always helps, right? I told myself it would. I smoked and jumped in the car to go to drill. Here's the problem: I was completely obliterated. I had no sense of direction, probably didn't even know at that moment where I was going. I was dressed in my BDU (which stands for battle dress uniform), but I was out of it. I must have passed out or something because the next thing I knew, I smashed into a vehicle in front of me.

Guess who came? Cops. I still really didn't have a sense of what was going on in my environment. I didn't fight them at first. I must've just sat there talking to myself. Must've sounded like gibberish. Apparently, to the cops, I sounded Arabic. I had a Koran in my Tahoe with me and I was wearing BDUs speaking gibberish before eight in the morning on a Saturday. What would you have thought? They thought I must be some kind of extremist. I was so high I couldn't tell them I was just a soldier. They tased me. Hog-tied me in the vehicle. I had open wounds from being hog-tied and a footprint on my face for a couple of days.

I spent a little time in a padded room while they sorted through my identification. My brother came to my rescue. He bailed me out of jail. I got evicted from my new place for not paying the rent.

The next couple of months were relatively calm. I started dating this girl because my wife moved away and wouldn't talk to me. She was dating other guys, and I didn't see why I needed to be lonely. I scared my girlfriend one time, though, when I was high on PCP. I started freaking out and broke a mirror with my hand in front of her. It was a stupid thing to do, and I felt stupid afterward. I was also glad that I didn't accidentally hurt her. I felt dumb for taking PCP instead of taking care of her. We decided to go to a bar that night for food, but once we got there, I decided that I wasn't hungry. I would rather wait in the car and smoke more. So I told her to meet me in the car. I thought I was being so logical because she could drive since she wasn't under the influence, and I could sit in the car and get high and I wouldn't have consequences. Funny thing about being high, though. You forget to think.

So while I was sitting in the car waiting for her, I decided that I had time to drive around and say hello to my biological mother. She lived in the area, and I could just pop in and say hi to her while I waited for my girlfriend. I was being social. And stupid. I drove right by a cop and got a DUI.

I got another DUI right around that same time period, although for that one I called the cops myself. I crashed into a parked vehicle and decided to play it straight. Unfortunately, I couldn't play it sober and they weren't fooled. DUI number three.

I had crashed up my Tahoe so many times that the next crash happened to my girlfriend's Lincoln Navigator. I was high on PCP and tried to drive into a lake. Maybe I was trying to hurt myself. I don't know. I can't say for sure what I was thinking. I drove over a median into incoming traffic, hit two trees, and another parked vehicle with people in it. I fought the cops that time and had more damage to my body from fighting the cops than I did from the accident.

Overall, I would say I had some definite problems with PCP. Bad things happened to me every time I used it. Some bad things happened that didn't involve the police, like I would be unresponsive and pass out. I woke up a couple of times in the hospital. One time I fell down the stairs in my apartment. Cracked open the area right above my eye, but didn't have major damage. Another time I climbed up a tree in the woods and was hanging off a branch about twenty-five feet up in the air. I was out of my mind. I was definitely looking for complete obliteration.

Hyperarousal

I had a hard time finding work because of all the drug use and legal issues. I had to work, though, and one opportunity opened up that seemed pretty good. There was this restaurant that relocated to another city, established new ownership, and had to start up from scratch. Since they were starting from scratch, they needed help setting up shop. It was fun because I got to help with construction and put together the toys and play equipment. It was one of those restaurants that focuses on children and children's parties? Like a Chuck E. Cheese's, but more upscale than that.

Putting together the restaurant was pretty interesting. I was like a game technician. Hosting children's parties was not exactly what I wanted to be doing with my life. I did it, though. I hosted several parties. So when a child had a birthday party or something, it was my job to be the guide of the party. I would tell them when it was time to eat and when it was time to play. The energy of the kids was fun, but I needed something more. If the choice was between hosting children's parties or deciding to do something else with my life, I had to choose something else. In fact, I'd rather be back at war than hosting these parties.

I got very agitated about going back to Iraq. Things at home were so off that I needed to get back to make things right. I knew when I left Iraq the first time that I wasn't ready, and I wasn't. I asked my National Guard unit if other deployments were about to happen. I was willing to be a part of another unit or anything. I just had to get out of here. War was better than this.

There has long been a link between symptoms associated with traumatic events and substance use. Using substances may provide immediate relief for problematic symptoms associated with trauma. For example, persons struggling with memories that make them feel edgy and tense may seek out substances to help their minds veer away from unpleasant memories. Likewise, someone may decide that taking a sleeping pill or using large amounts of alcohol may help her fall asleep. Anyone who has had an especially grueling day can understand the tendency to want to unwind by having a glass of wine or a beer. Unfortunately, in the case of severe trauma, a glass of wine or a beer will not provide the same type of relief as it would for someone who has been stuck in traffic for the past hour and would like to unwind. Severe trauma would require long-term and almost constant inebriation to help ease anxiety. Therein lies the problem: To use substances to treat symptoms of PTSD, one would have to use copious amounts of substances and may become addicted. Once a person is addicted to substances, treatment of PTSD becomes exceedingly more complicated as it is likely that symptoms of PTSD have not improved.

It is sometimes the case that substance use problems develop before the incidence of trauma, and the impaired judgment and behavior associated with substance use place the person at increased risk for traumatic events (e.g., sexual assault or motor vehicle accident). This individual has complicated his substance use disorder by adding PTSD to his list of problems. It's also likely that having PTSD would not improve his substance use problem.

Although they may seem logical, approaches that involve treating the "original" problem (substance use or PTSD) with the expectation that the secondary problem will improve are generally not effective. Integrated approaches that treat both the trauma and the substance use at the same time, as well as their interactions, are the most effective. Unfortunately, the majority of our systems of care in the United States do not offer integrative approaches to PTSD and substance use disorders. Many patients are shuffled from one treatment to another or, worse, asked to get their other condition treated first. Imagine deciding to get treatment for PTSD only to be told that you should get your addiction treated first. It has happened that a person goes in for addiction treatment and then is told he should get treatment for PTSD instead.

In Alex's case, it would be important for him to see the big picture of how his traumatic experience in war triggered his misuse of substances.

Recovery: Life Is So Hard. Why Be Anything but Kind?

Ironically, to recover from the stress of being at war, I had to go back to war. It was a decision I made in order to find my life again. I worried about what another deployment would do to my situation and my health, but I needed to get out of there.

When I heard that I would be able to deploy with the National Guard to Afghanistan, effective June 2010, I was excited. I contacted the courts, and when I return from my deployment in June 2011, I will have to take several court-ordered classes and pay my fines. I will not have to spend any time in jail, though. I was really lucky. I am never making that mistake ever again. I am glad I pulled through it, and am not going to make any decision that would hurt my forward progress ever again.

I beat myself up still over the decisions I made after my first deployment. I shouldn't have done that. That was rock bottom for me. I was in and out of jail for a couple of months and it was inexcusable. I have no excuses for my behavior. It was completely unprofessional and I was out of my lane. I'm very thankful that I didn't hurt anyone and that I have another chance. My path could have really been altered had I hurt another person while driving around under the influence. I shouldn't have done that.

I have made decisions about what I'm going to do with myself when I get back from this second deployment. First, I am not going to use substances. I don't need to and they didn't do me any good. In fact, everything got much worse every time I used. Let's be real. Every time I used, my life got bad.

The second thing I am going to do is go back to school full-time. I have already started the process for the GI Bill, which would help me pay for school. I have plans. I'd like to study business and/or psychology. Counseling. That might sound ironic since I had so much counseling as a kid, but I think I have a lot to offer troubled teenagers. I can help them not go down the road I went down.

You know, my troubles started when I was a teenager, but they were really exacerbated by my deployment. All of my issues got worse. I wish I had had someone to turn to that could have helped me through it at the time, but I didn't. It's my chance to help others, though. I can do for them what I needed myself.

I am into physical fitness right now too. I do that for my own benefit. It is for myself. I would rather use my energies to help people find their lives, not their fitness. You can find out all sorts of stuff about training and physical fitness on the Internet. You know, you can Google to find out fitness information, but you cannot find your life on Google.

I've been practicing a new lifestyle over here at war. I am practicing being positive and helpful to others. Over here, the big issue is morale. People start to get down on the situation or feel like they need to have some control over something. That negativity starts to take over. I would rather think about positive things. I think I can be helpful to others when they start to get negative. I try to be positive every day. It is not hard because I am thankful. It wasn't that long ago soldiers had to live in foxholes and didn't have roofs over their heads. I have lived in worse environments than the one I am in now right here in Afghanistan. We could be in the field. But we are in the barracks with a roof over our heads. I am grateful for what we have. This is where I can make a change and lead by example.

The two things I say most often are "we are alive" and "we are in a safe area." When we have to travel and do our thing, it's not generally considered "safe," but back at the barracks, we're OK. This whole situation we are currently in is temporary. It is not permanent. We will not always be sitting here in Afghanistan. All of this will pass.

Like today, for example, one of the guys got down and started to complain about certain individuals. It's hard because we are living in a confined area. Some individuals are not as neat as they could be. It's trifling in some circumstances. You know, it's appropriate to clean up after yourself. So in this case, this guy walked in with me, saw the mess, and said, "What the fuck? Fucking can't deal with this shit. I'm going to find out who did this and get their fucking ass in here to clean this mess up."

I looked around and thought, "I know who made the mess, but what does it matter?"

I said, "Listen, there is no solution. We're not here to police who does what mess, and we can't even always know who did what because new guys are in and out of here all the time. As long as you clean up after yourself and you lead by example, that's what matters."

"Man, I don't want to come back here and live in a mess. People have jobs and they are supposed to do them," he said.

I said, "That's negative thinking, man, and it's not going to get you anywhere except pissed off. Do your part, and that's all you can do."

We sat there on a bunk looking around. I heard him sigh as he sat next to me. I know he heard me and that's good. No point getting stuck in the negative.

He said, "I can't wait to get out of this place."

I said, "We're here now, and I'm glad I am sitting right here with you."

He sighed again.

I know he's feeling a little better. And that's how I can do my part.

Morale is a big problem right now. We're over here for a long time, but it's not a permanent situation. We have our children back home and we have people who need us. It's our job to make things better. And to be positive. I've been down a lot of rough roads in my life. And believe it or not, this isn't one of them.

As long as we are blessed with another day, we have a choice to start out fresh. Might be a process to dig out of that hole that we dug for ourselves, but at least we got the opportunity to start climbing. It's a good thing.

I still have circumstances back at home to deal with. I know that. I can't laugh yet. There are no excuses. I'm not sure I can explain it, but I am so grateful I am where I am right now today. I am grateful I got through it. It's my chance to make things right.

It's important that people understand I made bad decisions and I am owning up to the consequences of those decisions. I'm trying to

CHAPTER 4

Disaster: Ray's Story

Before Trauma: **The Love of Water**

This is not the hurricane story you saw on TV.

It doesn't take long speaking to Ray to know he has lived his whole life in the South. It's in his voice, his phrases, and the engaging way he has of drawing you in as though he's a long-term member of the family. The voice is melodic, yet deep and rich. A voice that says, "Hey there, girl, how are you?" This statement at the beginning of a conversation is as embracing as a hug. A big bear hug. A cuddly bear, though, not one of those mean ones. The kind of voice that has you contemplating sharing your darkest secrets, as you would with your closest friend.

When talking of his darker days, Ray speaks with a sad tone—a tone of grief so deep, the sound reminds you of being in a church as a child. A feeling of deep sorrow spears your heart. But when he talks about his childhood, he speaks with a lighter tone, one that resonates carefree and untroubled days. He speaks of his childhood as though that life were long ago and connections made then do not necessarily pertain to his current situation.

Christmases at our house were strange. We never spent Christmas at home. We would travel to my dad's parents' house at the farm on

Christmas Eve and my mom's parents' house on Christmas day. I grew up in Nashville, Tennessee, and my dad's parents' house was about ninety miles southwest in Wayne County. The farm had been my grandparents' before they sold it in 1916. Then in 1960, my father was able to help my grandfather buy the farm back. Many of my early memories occurred on that farm.

That was where I got my first real bicycle, a spider bicycle with five speeds and a banana seat. No training wheels on that bike. It was purple. I sat there and picked through the entire Sears catalog when I was seven years old to find the bike I wanted. Santa brought it to me on the farm on Christmas morning. It wasn't exactly the one I had picked out, but close enough. Boy, that bike meant freedom. It was the best toy ever. That bike meant that I was a big boy. No training wheels. I was free. And the bike represented my freedom.

In those days, kids were actually pretty free to roam and play. It's not like that now. Now you'd get charged with neglect, but then we would only get called back to the house when it was time for supper. And even then, our mother would want us to get out of her hair after supper. She didn't worry about what was happening to us. We knew all of our neighbors, and she didn't have to worry about things like parents do now.

It was also on that farm that I had a pony. I was the oldest grandson, and I rode that pony on weekends. I would go to those horse shows on that pony.

As I was the oldest grandson, my grandmother used to tell me that it was my duty to go to college and study to become an engineer. I never even realized that I had a choice in the matter because she drilled it into me that I was going to college to be an engineer. There was no other choice for me.

I had a great childhood. My father helped me with all the Cub Scout and Boy Scout activities. He didn't really do much else with me, but he was there for scouting.

My mother's family was a little different. My mother's family was big. She was one of eight children, four girls and four boys in that order. Each child had about two children, which meant there were twenty grandchildren, sixteen parents, and two grandparents each Christmas day for food. Imagine feeding all of those people? We had to do it in shifts. We were a big ole Southern family. The children all ate in the living room, and the men ate in the kitchen. The women served us. Only when we were all done eating were the women allowed to sit at the table and eat their dinner. That was the way things were done.

It was a big day when I was allowed to join the men in the kitchen for Christmas dinner. I remember that day well. I was about fifteen or sixteen years old, and now officially a man. That day, the turkey tasted better than ever. The men at the dinner table talked throughout the feast. Politics, sports, all of it. I was a man and part of the conversation. My opinion mattered now.

Well, except on what I would study at college. I went to college and became an engineer. Just as was expected of me.

Favorite Memory

When I was thirty-one years old, I bought my first big boat. It was a thirty-seven-foot sailboat. I lived in Texas but bought the sailboat in North Palm Beach, Florida. I was at the Hall of Fame Marina with the boat broker, and we sailed down to Fort Lauderdale.

I will never forget that feeling. The peace and quiet of the water commingling with the noise of the wind blowing in my face. The bright white of the boat contrasting with the blue water, letting me know that boat was mine. I had made it. My dreams were coming true. The life I wanted for myself was going to be mine. I had my own big sailboat. I had already hired out a captain to sail it to Houston for me, and everything was set.

When we pulled into the slip in Fort Lauderdale, I knew I had arrived. Life was as good as I had always expected, and my dreams were coming true. There I was on my own boat sailing into a slip in Fort Lauderdale, Florida. I was a man. I had made it.

No one warned me that my own little sailboat would pull into a slip right next to another sailboat. A bigger sailboat. A bigger sailboat by a ton! My little ole sailboat pulled into a slip right smack-dab next to an eighty-five-foot yacht.

It was like that yacht looked down at me and said, "You've made step one, junior. Now sit down and shut up." My eighty-thousand-dollar sailboat next to a four-million-dollar yacht, I didn't quite cut it anymore. But I'll never forget the feeling of sailing down to the marina in my new boat. Just the idea, albeit for a short time, that I had made it. That was great.

I lived on that boat for five years. It was literally the best time of my life living on that boat. I worked at a chemical plant during the day as an engineer and would come home to my boat at night. I would fix myself a drink and sit in the cockpit. It was so peaceful there. You could hear no noise except the birds and the slapping of the water on the hull. The wind would be blowing, but in a good way. A way that made you feel like the wind was cutting through you peacefully. A quiet hello. The kind of wind that offers to take away stress and troubles. Gently. My life did not suck. It did not suck at all.

I was able to compete in sailboat races in my boat for fun. I competed in many of them just for the sheer pleasure of being on my boat. I met my wife in a boat race in 1991. Told her that I was living on my boat and she said, "My shoes won't even fit on that boat. I ain't living on that boat." That was the end of my time living on the boat. Onward to a home on the coast in Gulfport, Mississippi.

In Every Life, a Little Shit Must Fall

My wife had a blocked colon. We cracked jokes about it, but it was a little hard to do that because she was in quite a bit of pain. Her physician scheduled for her to have surgery on her colon and while they were working on her, they found a big lump on her ovary. So they cut it out.

For me, that was that. They found a lump on her ovary. That had been what was causing all that pain. Didn't have a blocked colon.

That's good. Had a lump instead. OK, fine. They cut it right out of there. Things should have been fine then. Except the damned thing grew back.

I wanted to ask "Why?" I asked "Why?" a lot, even though I knew there wasn't an answer. She knew it was growing back because the pain for her was excruciating when it was growing. It would attach itself to a blood vessel, see, and cause hemorrhaging.

I knew she was in pain because she would be quiet. We'd be sitting there watching TV together, and she would just sit and be quiet. Wouldn't say a word. That meant she was in pain. She would sit and chew Lortabs. That's when I knew.

I would sit with her and watch TV. That was OK with me. She and I sitting together. I learned to deal with it. I couldn't change anything. But I didn't like it. I would sit and ask myself, "Why would anyone want to die?" That's the thing I don't understand about suicide. I don't understand the concept of suicide. Nothing is really that bad, and nothing is worse than dying. You should cherish what there is to cherish. It's like that concept of the glass being half empty or half full. To me, the glass is half full. I mean, really, things could always get worse.

I'm not very religious, but I believe there is a higher power. When my wife was diagnosed with ovarian cancer, I said to God, "Yes sir. You have my attention." She had ovarian cancer for eight years. Every time they cut it out, the tumor would grow back. It grew back three times. God had my attention.

I don't care for organized religion. I do believe in God, but I don't care much for some of those preachers. I guess you could say that I believe in God, but I wonder about man. I don't like any preacher that says, "I will save your soul. All you have to do is send me that there little hundred dollars." I don't think God works that way.

And those Catholics. Whoa. Those were some evil people in the Dark Ages. They didn't get all that art by themselves, you know. They stole it.

So that's my life. I am a married man. I love my life. I love my job. I love my boat. We live in a big, beautiful home off the coast of Mississippi. I have good friends and a wonderful family. My wife has a fairly serious illness, and we are going to fight our way through it.

And that's how my life was until little Ms. Katrina came along.

TRAUMA: Come Hell or High Water

We live half a block off the beach, sandwiched between the beach and the harbor. The south part of the house faces the beach and the north faces the harbor. We were not worried about Katrina. Our house was built in 1911 and we were eighteen feet above sea level. Our house had already been through a couple of events and hadn't gone down yet. Hurricane Camille was our benchmark for hurricanes, and we had absolutely no water damage from Camille. So this here Katrina should have been just fine for us. We were just having us a little storm.

When we heard that Katrina was coming, we prepared for the storm. We decided that we would stay because we didn't want anyone to steal from us. When Camille hit, looters took advantage of the situation and stole from my wife's grandmother. I didn't want anyone stealing from my wife, so we stayed put. We took care of business in terms of preparing for the storm, meaning that we stocked up on water and canned goods, boarded up the windows, made sure the generator was running, made sure all four cars were full of gas, and picked up the lawn. A lawn chair can make for an excellent projectile during a storm. So can a lawnmower, for that matter. So we took care of business that morning. But we weren't worried about the storm itself. We went through the motions of taking care of the things we needed to take care of to get through the storm.

It's ridiculous to think about now. We made sure that all four of our cars had gas. Why would we do that when there were only two of us to drive them? I'm not sure exactly what we thought we were going to do with four cars and two drivers.

My wife is an animal lover, so she was mildly concerned about her animals. We had a big black lab that we rescued from Tennessee, a cat that adopted us a couple of years prior, and a parrot.

We spent the entire night before the storm hit checking the weather channel. During storms, you have to live by that weather channel. The national and local news don't quite cut it in terms of giving you the overall picture of the storm, so you have to check the weather channel every couple of hours. It seems like we watched that station all night long that night.

When we woke up in the morning, the water was about ten feet higher, but everything was still OK. I was thinking that things were going to be OK. About that time, my wife decided to go outside to have a closer look at the beach. She walked over to the front door, opened it, walked onto the porch facing the beach, came back in, and screamed, "We need to get the fuck out of here! The roof is coming off the house!"

I watched her. The first thing she grabbed was her meds. She picked up the cat and put him in the carrying case, put the leash on the dog, and put some clothes in a bag. We'd agreed to go to her cousin's house when the storm hit.

Her cousin grew up during the McCarthy period and their house is a concrete bunker. "The Russians are coming any minute now" kind of concrete bunker. Perfect for a storm. And that's where we were headed.

I told her, "I'll get the bird and his food and I'll meet you up there."

I was stumbling around a little wondering what else to grab, but I was not panicking. I was thinking, "I'll be back here in a half an hour, so I don't need to grab much." I was wearing Bermuda shorts, a T-shirt, and tennis shoes. I saw my college ring sitting on the dresser in my bedroom and decided to put it on. I got the birdcage and the food and moved onto the front porch.

As I pulled the door open, I was thinking again, "I'll be back here in thirty minutes. There is nothing to worry about." I turned back to look at my house before I closed the door and I watched the wind tear out the back part of my house.

I was aware now that everything was going to get wet. This was going to be a mess. The house would be fine, but it would be a pain in the neck to clean it up. I have insurance, so I knew it was not going to be a problem to take care of things, but, God, was this going to be a mess.

As I looked down the street, I could see the water coming. Oh, crap. I mean crap. Now this was all going to be crap. It wasn't just going to be wet, it was going to be wet Sheetrock. All of our books were going to be ruined. It was going to be a mess. The water was coming.

We spent about an hour and a half over at her cousin's house in the concrete bunker. Their house was up at twenty-four feet above sea level, and the storm surged to reach almost twenty-four feet. So we were able to stand on their front porch during most of the surge and watch. It is amazing to see the water rise. You can't think about much. Just sit back and watch that rising water and think, "Wow, that's incredible." It's a steady buildup.

I saw one of the columns from the front of my house floating down the street. Things were now bad.

It seemed to happen slowly, but also fast. About a half hour of rising water and then it started to ease up and go back down. Within an hour and a half, the water was back down, so we decided to go back to our house and survey the damage.

We didn't talk much walking back to our house. It was too hard to talk. There was too much to attend to under our feet and all around us. We had to climb over and around the debris. Our house was a couple of houses away, about 125 yards, as the houses aren't small, but it was like picking your way through a minefield. We had to look down to make sure that we didn't step on a nail sticking out of a piece of wood. The wood was wet and slippery, so we were sliding around and holding on and trying to move forward.

At the same time, I kept looking up to see our house. I didn't see it yet, but it was hard to look because there was also too much under and around where I was trying to step. None of it was stuff that was there a couple of hours ago. This was like a debris field. Everything was all over the place.

But something caught my attention. It looked like my chair. I didn't say anything because even though it was bizarre, I saw something that was even more bizarre.

"Isn't that the cushion on the wingback chair that your mother embroidered?"

My wife didn't answer even though she was looking at the cushion. She seemed as shocked as I felt. Also, I was looking for my house. I wondered if I was going in the right direction or if I'd gotten turned around a bit. I knew it should have been right there where I was looking, but I hadn't seen it yet.

Well, how in the hell did those jeans get up there? It appeared like a pair of Martin's jeans were stuck in a tree. It was hard to look up. It was impossible to stop looking down because things were all over the place.

"There's your Miata."

My wife's Miata was sitting there in the neighbor's yard. That was definitely not where we left it. Yet it was full of gas. We loaded up all four cars full of gas in case we needed them. I was aware that I couldn't even find the road because the road was covered. Covered in houses and trees and boats and cars and chairs and clothes and all sorts of broken pieces.

Well, that house ought to have been right there. And I didn't see the house. I could see the concrete driveway that led up to the guest-house, but the house was gone. Literally gone. There was nothing there. I was standing there looking at the house, and I was not really having any thoughts at all. Just wondering how the entire house could be gone. Even the foundation. It was rubble. But not even a lot of rubble. It was gone. My wife's Suburban was in the driveway.

The day was sunny and clear. It was around noon. The storm was just there and had passed us now. It was hot, felt about ninety degrees, and there was a slight breeze in the air. Beautiful day really. But it appeared as though my house was gone. I saw a twenty-two-foot fishing boat wrapped around a pine tree. That was not there before.

I walked around the yard several times. Looking. I couldn't seem to think anything except feel this numb awareness that this was not a dream. I was not going to wake up and find my house put back together. The house had literally been swept out into the Gulf. There were tidbits of the house and our stuff here and there, but it was gone.

I thought this same thought again as I walked into what was my backyard. There were pieces of things left here and there. Eventually I found my diesel truck in the gully. That's a heavy truck to push all the way over to that gully.

It was quiet out there. There was no one around. The people were gone. There was hardly any movement, but my wife was next to me, looking around. Our cousins were looking around. No one was talking. There wasn't a thing to say except the occasional, "Look at that thing there! How did it get there?" Disbelief.

We spent the rest of the day picking through the debris. We spent the night at our cousins'. I don't think we even ate much. Everyone had stocked their pantries with food and water for the storm, but no one told us that our stock would float away in the Gulf.

No one could drive up and help us because the roads were full of debris. We couldn't drive to get help because our cars were ruined. There weren't any stores or anything open anyway. And even if they were, there wasn't any electricity. None of us had any power.

Four cars full of gas. None of them ran. Hell, I couldn't even find one of them. Didn't occur to me that the cars would move around. That they'd get soaked. That the road would be gone. For the life of me, I couldn't figure what I was thinking, making sure all of them were full of gas.

Debris

The four of us were sitting in a circle picking through dirt and rubble. Broken boards were everywhere. No one was talking. The day was hot. Steaming hot. I had on the same clothes I wore the day before because it didn't occur to me to pack anything. My wife packed a bag, but she was always a little smarter than me. I thought I'd be back in thirty minutes. What the hell did I need another pair of shorts for?

"Here's another one of your forks, Heather."

She didn't look into her cousin's eyes as she took back the fork. Stared down at it for a second and put it into a pile next to more of her forks. Spoons. Some of her jewelry had been found. A couple of gold chains, her father's wedding band. Katrina took all the damned knives with her. Hollow handles.

I sat in my house just nights earlier ranting that no looters were going to come and steal my wife's silver and china. We'd stay through the storm. I said, "I'm not going to let them come in here and dig through our belongings like they're all for the taking. I will not let them come in here and steal from us." Hollow handles float. Didn't think about Katrina stealing from us. Didn't even occur to me. I was thinking about those looters.

I picked through the debris trying not to think anymore. Boards go in a pile over here. Pick up this board and bring it over here. Pick up this other board and bring it over here. Don't think about the fact that you're sweating like a pig and have no other shorts. Can't just drive over to the Big and Tall to buy more shorts today because there is no road. The car is flooded. There is no electricity, and probably no store. Don't think about sweating in your shorts. The washer and dryer at our cousins' house are not going to work without power or water, so your shorts are going to stay a damned mess. Don't think about your wife's eyes when she looked down at one of her treasured silver forks. She ran her fingers over each tine, caressing them as she would a young child's face. Her forks were being returned to her, but her face was full of loss.

As I picked up another board, careful to watch for the nails sticking out at every angle, I heard my wife talking with her cousin.

"We should stop and eat lunch soon."

"Why don't we work on this area for just a bit longer, and then we'll take a break."

"Feels like we might be sitting here cleaning up forever."

"We need about six big dumpsters to come and take all the rubble away."

"But we can't just cart it all away. We keep finding stuff of ours in here."

"Oh, I know, dear. I just meant I wish there were an easier way to pick through this rubble. It feels like we're sitting in the middle of a war zone where everything was bombed to pieces. It feels like insanity here."

It was a bit like a war zone. Not that I've ever been to a war zone, but I imagine this was what it might look like. Except the smell. It smelled pretty good there. Wet, but a clean ocean smell. I bet a war zone doesn't smell like the wet ocean.

It was hotter than blazes that day. Couldn't catch a break.

I needed to sit down. We were all taking a break in a minute anyway to grab some lunch, so I figured I should just sit there with them and pick through the little parts. We'd partially cleared away a small area in our front yard, or what was our front yard, to dig up whatever we could find. Had been finding a few pieces here and there. As I sat, I couldn't help but glance over to the ocean. It was beautiful out there. The waves were peacefully coming in. I could hear them. Hard to believe the water rose like a monster the day before. Our house was completely underwater. It washed away. I was picking through dirt for remnants of my life inside the house. It was just a house. But it was my house. And my house was gone. I was picking for remnants of my life. A fork. A spoon. A broken chair. Found a pair of my jeans earlier that morning. I couldn't wear them. Hotter than the hinges on the gates of hell out there. And my shorts were filthy.

Our cousin started to hold something up in his hand. It was dirty but recognizable. For just a moment, I held my breath. Then I breathed deeply in and out. My wife took it from him and held it close to her body. Close to her heart. She was also breathing differently. No breath, and then a big, deep one. Her mouth quivered. She was clearly holding back tears, but they started streaming down her face anyway. I knew she was remembering the way her and her mama used to taunt each other about this bracelet. It was an anniversary gift from her daddy to her mama. I think it was their fortieth wedding anniversary. Something like that anyway. Her daddy had given that bracelet to her mama. There's about fourteen carats of diamonds in that bracelet. My wife wanted it. She was going to inherit it after her mama passed, and they would tease each other. Her mama would say that she could only have it after she was dead and gone. Not before.

So my wife would joke. She would say to me in front of her, "I think she passed. I get that bracelet now. Is she passed?"

I'd say, "Yeah, I think she's passed."

And they'd laugh. The bracelet meant love. Family.

We never even realized we might have lost it until it was dug up right there. Somehow the loss resonated still. She was still holding it in her hand. She was not moving and was looking off into the ocean. She must have been remembering joking of her mama's passing. She must have been feeling like her mama was right here with her right now. Damn, I'm glad that bracelet came back to where it belonged.

I am glad her mama's bracelet is back, but we never did find my grandfather's watch. It was an Eagle Scout model and was in the jewelry box in our dresser. Must still be somewhere out at sea.

Work

I couldn't call my parents and let them know that I was OK. I left my cell phone in my bedroom. Thought I'd be back in thirty minutes. Cell phone, gone. Hell, my bedroom was gone.

As I was sitting there looking around at the mess, I thought about my phone. I was getting tired of that mess of rubble. Crap everywhere. I didn't have my clothes. I didn't have my phone. I didn't have any knives. There wasn't much water to drink. It was hotter than hell out there. I couldn't find one of my cars. My house was in pieces or in the Gulf somewhere. In tiny little pieces. I couldn't call work and let them know that I wouldn't be in for a while. Hell, I worked in New Orleans, so I didn't even know if work still existed. Our baby pictures were gone. Mardi Gras outfits. Gone.

What I remember of that time is a lot of quiet crying. Particularly when we found something that we thought was gone forever.

Hurricane Katrina hit on a Monday morning on August 29, 2005. Winds were around 125 miles per hour when the hurricane landed on the coast off Louisiana. Almost two thousand people lost their lives as a result of Katrina, and it is considered the costliest hurricane in U.S. history. Ninety percent of structures within a half mile of the coast in Mississippi were completely leveled by the hurricane. Some estimates suggest that the storm surge brought water as far as six miles inland.

The destruction in the New Orleans area alone caught an enormous amount of media attention primarily because of the number of individuals whose lives were so profoundly affected by the destruction. Flooding that resulted from the breaching of the levees caused an unprecedented amount of damage. The majority of individuals living in the New Orleans area stayed during the storm, either because they tried to evacuate too late (i.e., after the levees broke and there was nowhere to go) or because they did not realize they needed to leave, had no means of leaving, and had nowhere to go. People either were taken to the Superdome (where conditions quickly deteriorated because families had difficulty finding each other, toilets broke, food and water were scarce, and violence was rampant), or were bused all across the country (which was also a nightmare because they didn't even necessarily know where they were being taken, had no phones, and had no way to get in touch with their families, whose whereabouts they often did not know). The death toll was high, either directly related to the storm or because people with medical conditions did not have access to what they needed to survive. Recovery efforts in New Orleans were overwhelmed by the extent of residents' needs and the inadequacy of available resources.

The Breaking Point

Many individuals cope with trauma by avoiding memories of the traumatic event, yet in some situations avoiding memories of the event can be difficult and even impossible. In the face of natural disasters, such as hurricanes or large-scale earthquakes, painful reminders of the event are ubiquitous, and the impact of the disaster hits upon virtually every aspect of life. Families, health, homes, work, life, roads, communities, power, water—all damaged, if not destroyed.

For the majority of us, coping with devastation on this scale would prove overwhelming. We would need to rely heavily on resources and support beyond our own internal reserves. It would not surprise anyone that disasters such as Hurricane Katrina result in emotional overload. This may be particularly difficult for individuals who tend to rely only on themselves to cope. We all know people who are prone to make statements such as, "I can deal with it" or "I like to handle things on my own, I don't want anyone's help."

Emotional strain becomes even more difficult given the length of time that victims of disasters must cope. It is one thing to endure this type of strain for one day, but victims of disasters must cope with the consequences of the event for days, weeks, months, and even years. Chronic strain on this scale may be seen to resemble torture.

In any introductory psychology course, students are taught about stress and the impact of repeated stressors on the human body. It is often not the severity of the stressor that breaks down an individual but the repetition of the stressor. For example, many people would say that a dead car battery is an annoying stressor. You accidentally leave your car lights on one night and discover the next morning that the battery has no "juice." This would be stressful. Perhaps stressful enough that you shout curse words up into the air. Maybe your heart starts to beat a little faster, breathing becomes shallow, and the muscles in your jaw and hands and back tighten. Some people might even contemplate kicking the car (or worse). One dead car battery might be perceived as stressful. But imagine that the car battery died several times in one week. The first time the battery died, it may have been annoying. The second, super annoying. The third, beyond belief, and anytime after that it is just ridiculous. You likely would kick the car. Maybe even several times. It's virtually guaranteed that you would utter curse words. But that is about a car battery. Now imagine the impact a more severe stressor may have on an individual, such as finding out that a beloved relative fighting cancer has ended up septic in the hospital after a round of chemotherapy. Treating the disease resulted in a poor and potentially fatal outcome for the family member. Then imagine that it happens again, and again. That first time alone would be traumatic. The impact of the stressor on the individual physiology becomes more severe through repeated incidents.

(As an aside, my husband, also a psychologist, read this section and said the example of a car battery was absurd. He indicated that no male would become stressed over problems with a car battery. A man would merely deal with the problem and move on. I, however, have witnessed men dealing with car-related issues by kicking and cursing. My husband's opinion was included here to illustrate how we also overestimate our capacity to cope.)

So a natural disaster would, in essence, create a wonderful opportunity for us to learn about how we cope, and how much strength we have on reserve. By extension, a natural disaster also creates an opportunity for us to learn how poorly we cope, and how little pain and discomfort we can endure.

It is interesting, too, how many of us will admit that we feel capable of handling severe stress in the heat of the moment, but that little things make us crazy. I heard a comic recently demonstrating just this point. He said he often contemplated suicide—not about the big things, only the little ones. He indicated that he recently thought about killing himself because he had promised his girlfriend he would make a pie for Thanksgiving.

Repetitive stress doesn't have to be the same stressor repeated. It can also result when many stressors are introduced in a short period of time. For example, imagine your car battery dying on the way to the grocery store to buy carpet cleaner because your dog has suddenly come down with a vicious case of diarrhea. And you suspect your child has another ear infection and is screaming at the top of her lungs in the backseat of the car on a Sunday, and you know your doctor will not see her until tomorrow. And you are not entirely sure if you will continue to have adequate health insurance because your employer is talking about downsizing. And you know they have not been particularly fond of your output for the past couple of months because you have been sidetracked with a sick child at home (repeated ear infections). And your spouse has been crabby lately because he recently found out that his mother might have a terminal disease. Life can be stressful.

All of us have learned to cope with stress, and we each have developed our own repertoire for coping with stress (in the field, we may refer to this as "tools in the toolbox"). Examples of coping skills or "tools" include talking, crying, exercise, drinking, attending a worship service, praying, watching TV, yelling, cooking, eating, sleeping, making lists, laughing, arguing, spending money, doing art, and listening to or making music. Coping with a grand-scale disaster not only would overwhelm the toolbox but also would probably limit access to preferred coping skills. For example, an individual may love golf. She may find that her Sunday golf game is the perfect antidote to a stressful workweek. Personally, it is hard to imagine trying to get a tiny little ball into a tiny little hole with a titanium stick as calming, yet some people love golf for combating stress. Access to golf greens was probably extremely limited for months or years after Katrina. Thus, grand-scale disasters often demand that we look further for help.

Admittedly, some individuals, as shown on television news reports, had no problem demanding help from others, and none too soon. Others, probably not shown on television news, had difficulty asking for help.

Likewise, some individuals focused on restoring and rebuilding what was lost while others were more likely to relocate. Some individuals fixated on emotions during tragedies, while others worked hard to dissociate from negative emotions.

There is no one right way to cope with a disaster, and what works for one individual may not work for another. The challenge is for each individual to find the right balance of coping that works for him- or herself: the right balance of emotions and figuring out how to use those emotions for personal good and the greater good. For example, feeling uncomfortable in chaos motivated many individuals to clean up debris after Katrina. Others were enraged that there was debris and demanded that the National Guard and government come in to clean up their neighborhoods.

Sometimes negative emotions are unproductive. Yet sometimes it is appropriate and healthy to be angry, even enraged. Emotions can serve as signals for action. The trick is figuring out when, where, and how to act.

At the same time, it is generally unhealthy to avoid negative emotions. Many individuals work hard to avoid negative emotions at all costs. Some may use substances to numb feelings, while others redirect negative emotions into some other task. For the most part, the healthiest thing to do is figure out why you are feeling what you are feeling, feel it, decide what can be done about the situation, decide what to do, and act.

Let's return to Ray. Ray's two preferred coping techniques were avoidance and focusing on the positive. He did not like to dwell on the negative, and in fact he turned away from negative emotions and situations. When unpleasant events occurred in Ray's life, he had a tendency to move away from feeling pain and instead tried to focus on improving the situation. An example is when his wife developed ovarian cancer. Ray did not spend time dwelling on her illness but instead worked hard to make her life better. They did not talk about her pain, and he even spoke of how they joked about her disease. When the hurricane hit, it was virtually impossible for him to avoid stimuli associated with it. His home had literally floated out to sea and the majority of his possessions were either destroyed or lost. His neighborhood and community were destroyed, and along with them any semblance of control over the situation. Ray seemed to have no ability to maneuver around the situation. He had difficulty talking about negative experiences he endured during the cleanup process.

One of the most common experiences during a natural disaster is a profound sense of loss of control. So Ray decided to focus on rebuilding, both at home and at work. That was something he could control.

Looky Lous

Two days after the storm, we sat on our cousins' front porch, just where we sat when the storm surge happened. It was hot out and we had spent the morning and early afternoon gathering up debris. Boy, was it hot. Hot hot. We only had a limited amount of water, so the heat was a problem. I looked up and saw some of my friends from the yacht club walking up.

We all ran over and gave each other hugs. Big hugs. The ladies cried and hugged.

"We all got together to come find you. See if you were all doing OK," they said.

We started walking over to show them our place. No one said too much because they were looking around at all the mess.

"I'll be," someone exclaimed.

I saw some guy walking around my yard. I didn't recognize him and didn't know why he was there on my property. In fact, I thought, "What the hell is he doing on my property?" He was walking around by a bunch of rubble, and I could see that he was just about to step on a marble tabletop. I saw the tabletop under a bunch of other debris, and he was heading right for it.

In my mind, I was back in Mexico with my wife. I remembered finding that marble piece with her there. It was a nice trip, and she was so excited to find that piece. She knew just how she was going to use it. But she didn't anticipate the storm. That the tabletop would be sitting in the yard under a bunch of rubble with a strange man walking straight toward it. As he stood on top of it, I watched it break. I couldn't even speak as I watched it break. Wasn't there enough damage already? And what the hell was that guy doing on my property anyway?

Looky Lous. People walking around looking at destruction. What right do they have? Finally, I shouted, "Quit looking at my misery, asshole!"

I felt my friend's hand on my arm. It was a vivid moment. After spending a couple of days feeling mentally numb, it was great to get together with friends.

Work

Three days after the storm, I saw a guy walking down the street talking on a cell phone. Boy, did that look strange. He was wearing Bermuda shorts, a blue shirt, and tennis shoes. He was looking around at some of the mess and seemed to be talking about what he saw.

"Do you mind if I borrow your phone when you're done?" I said to him.

"Sure. You must have some people to call," he said.

"I sure do," I told him, thinking I should call my parents and let them know I was alive. I also had to call work and find out if I still had a job. I drove ninety minutes to work every day, to New Orleans. I had no idea how I was going to get to work. I had no idea if work was still there.

I dialed the phone number to my boss. He picked up and I said, "Hey, I'm calling to—"

"You're alive! Thank God. Get here as quick as you can. We've got work to do."

That's when I cried. It took me three days to be able to let it out, not even knowing that I was holding it in. And out it came. Big, huge tears. I was so grateful to have a job. I was kneeling on the pavement, weeping. I was halfway aware of the guy standing over me with his hand on my shoulder. I was looking around at all the crap and mess and rubble, and I couldn't help but feel an overwhelming sense of hope. Things sucked, but it was going to be OK. We could pull this back together. It was all still tough, but I was going to be able to pull things back together.

I told my boss I would be in as soon as I was physically able to get there. I looked up at the guy and said, "Thanks for the phone."

"No problem. I live a couple of blocks over and wanted to see what the coast looks like. Doesn't look good."

"No, it's not good over here."

I'm a civil engineer. I build chemical plants. We work on pipelines. We focus on leak detection and buried pipelines. I bet there's a shitload of work to do there too.

Insurance Claims

I had to call the insurance company to make a claim on the house. I was fairly confident that this was a matter of calling the company, putting in the claim, and giving the time and energy to getting the house back up and running. I was not worried about that part.

My guess was that they were busy on the phone with all sorts of families getting their claims in, and that they were feeling pretty stressed. But that's what would be expected in a storm of this nature. We were all here now to help each other out.

When I first talked to the company, the lady I spoke to was real nice. We had ourselves a little conversation, and she took down all of the information. I had to have someone from the insurance company come out and take pictures. "Ain't much left to take pictures of," I said, "but come on down and take pictures."

I understood that there might be some calculations that needed to get done. The house was four thousand square feet. There was a guesthouse. It was beachfront property. But, you know, come on down and document the disaster zone.

I was surprised and angry when I heard that they were not covering the claims on the house. They offered to cover one-third the price of the house. I called them up and said, "I can't replace my house for a third of its price."

The lady I was talking to, her name was Tanya, she said, "It's a problem of rising water. We are not able to cover any damages caused by rising water."

I said to her, as calmly as possible, "I stood there and saw with my own eyes the back of my house blow in. That would be a problem of wind. Wind. Not water."

She said, "If the damages were caused by rising water, we are not able to cover the losses for that."

I couldn't replace the house for that. The house was worth several times that much. My house was my wealth. I worked hard, saved money, bought property on the water, and was living the American dream in my home. It doesn't seem fair.

Months later, I remember having a conversation with my brother-in-law. We were able to drive up to Tennessee to have Christmas dinner with my baby sister and her family. That was nice, considering that we didn't have a home yet to live in. My brother-in-law seemed to believe that the insurance company was right not to cover claims.

He actually said that the people who owned the houses were all docs and lawyers anyway. That they could afford to rebuild. I couldn't believe he said that. People work hard in life for what they get.

Problem is that everyone thinks Katrina and associates it with New Orleans. People associate Katrina with the decades of thieving and dirty politicians of New Orleans. The politicians didn't keep the levees up to speed, and on account of that, the levees failed and New Orleans flooded.

I mean, come on, you live below sea level, dumbass. Leave. If you don't like living in the projects, get a job and then leave. People there had some control over the situation.

The Gulf Coast wasn't like that. People earned what they had and deserved what they had. It still takes my breath away to know that it could all float away. Right before your very eyes. And that no one would really care.

Help

What amazes me about the entire deal was how many people actually came to help. It was a snapshot of humanity. We are a cynical lot, but it is amazing how we can come together.

Heather's cousin, for example, got a deal worked out with Joe's Big and Tall shop. I lost all of my clothing, and I couldn't just go to Target to restock because I am a big person. I have to get clothes from special stores that cater to big men. This cousin was able to get six pairs of shorts and six T-shirts donated to me. I was so grateful to the person who donated the clothing to me. I don't even know who it was that contributed, but it was the nicest thing. I had been in my clothes for several days.

It still amazes me how smart Heather was to pack extra clothing for herself when we left the house that day. You will never know how smart that is until you spend a week or so sitting in the hottest heat cleaning up debris in one pair of shorts. Boy oh boy!

It occurs to me now that my wife may have secretly begged her cousin to help us out on some extra clothing for me. I had to have stunk.

Another out-of-the-blue, delightful offering came from a preacher upstate. He donated a tractor-trailer full of generators. The tractor-trailer showed up one day full of generators, gas cans, and oil to put in the generators. Didn't want even a thank-you in return. Those generators came in handy.

My cousin let me borrow his truck and I met my parents upstate so that I could have their extra truck from the farm. I didn't stay that long to visit, though. I had to get back to Heather right away. But the trip back was wonderful. It's amazing to have wheels again. It's a sense of freedom. Just like my first bicycle represented freedom. This extra truck gave me the ability to move around a little to help put things back into place.

Another one of our buddies brought stuff down from Tennessee.

We were putting things back together. I couldn't help but think about some of the folks who weren't so lucky. I still had a job, wheels, a generator, some clothing. One of our other friends wasn't so lucky. Like this one woman we knew. She is drop-dead gorgeous and used to go to church together with Heather. Her significant other owned a boat dealership. After the hurricane, no one was buying boats, and they had a hard time getting back on their feet.

It's amazing the sense of community after such devastation. One of my happiest memories after the storm was seeing our friends from the yacht club walk up to check on us and see if we were OK. I remember big smiles and hugs all around. But after the storm I was happy to see people I don't even like. Just seeing something familiar, even if it is someone you don't like, is great. It's familiar. It feels good to see them alive.

People flocked from all over the country to help us rebuild. Faith-based ministries drove people in to help. Children, really. Children came to help us rebuild. I remember a group of teenagers and young adults from Connecticut who came down to help us clean up and rebuild. There were piles of debris to be picked up. The kids got a FEMA [Federal Emergency Management Agency] trailer, lived there, and helped us clean up. They even made a video of their trip. I remember them interviewing my wife for their video.

I am amazed at all the goodwill. Children coming to help us clean up. Their energy was amazing. I remember that week well because Heather went to the doctor after the interview with the kids. The doctor gave us a good report. The tumor was shrinking. We finally got the right cocktail together to kill that monster. The tumor was shrinking.

Not only that, but there was an entire community coming in to help us clean up the mess. I am amazed at the generosity of people.

My wife died the following week. She died of a massive stroke caused by complications of chemotherapy and heart damage.

Grief

Now I sit here alone in a FEMA trailer. I sit here and think about the family that used to be in this trailer. We knew them. They were here for a short time but then decided that they wanted to rebuild their lives in Duluth, Minnesota. So we bought their place. We were going to rebuild our home and then sell this one once we had finished rebuilding.

Now it is me and the trailer. It is terribly quiet in here.

I think about our planned trip to Ireland this week. We planned on flying over to Ireland to replace some of the crystal that she had lost. We were going to visit the Waterford factory and tour around. That can't happen now. Hell, I don't need crystal now.

I look around this place and it's hard not to feel bad. I feel real bad. It's hard to even think.

RECOVERY: **The Power of Friends**

Compassion

The reality is that no matter how bad things are for you, there are always people in worse shape. I lived through that storm, and there were some people that didn't. I have other friends who lost their homes on the beach. I know another lady that took her mother and daughters and went to Disney World in Florida when they knew the storm was coming. They took off and left the dad at home to clean up the mess. When they realized how bad the storm was, they tried to come back home. On the drive home, a tractor-trailer ran them off the road. She is now paralyzed and in a wheelchair.

Circumstances can always be worse than what they are. Circumstances are worse for other people. There is no point spending time sitting around feeling sorry for yourself when at any moment things could be worse. I lost my home and my heart that year. Things can always get worse.

The Decision to Move Forward

Decisions to move forward happen randomly sometimes. Out of nowhere, you decide to restructure your life. It's not like I got out of bed on this particular morning and decided that today was the day I was going to change my life. But it so happens that on one random morning, about a year after Katrina hit, on my drive to work, I decided to change my life.

That's how it worked. One August morning on my drive to New Orleans, I changed my life.

Here is what happened.

It was a hot day. Some mornings you can tell that it is going to be a hot day outside when by eight in the morning, it is already steaming. I walked out of my trailer that morning and was sweating before I sat down in my car. Turned on the air-conditioning first thing. At eight I knew it was going to be a hot day out. Not even the birds were chirping. They were too busy sitting in the shade of a tree hoping the shade would last awhile longer. Couldn't waste their energies chirping to each other. All they'd say was, "Damn, it's hot out here" to each other anyway. And they already knew that.

These were my thoughts on this morning: I could tell that I wasn't happy anymore. My life needed to change. I began to realize I was holding on to things I didn't need to hold on to anymore. I needed to track backwards for a minute and remember what really mattered.

So what matters? What matters is that it's hot out today. My air-conditioning works in my new truck. That matters. I am not going to think about the fact that I had to buy a new truck that cost forty thousand dollars, and I still miss my old one that had three hundred thousand miles on it. I sure did love that truck. It wasn't old; I just drove it a lot. Insurance company only reimbursed me seven thousand for the loss. New one costs forty thousand. Guess that's just math. Insurance company math.

My wife is no longer here. That matters. But I can't change anything about that.

I'm supposed to close on our house soon. It's in the middle of probate.

Do I need to drive to New Orleans every day for work anymore? Am I supposed to continue to do this? I don't need the money. My savings was not tied up in the home. My house was paid off when Katrina hit and I wasn't in debt. I don't have debt now. I think I need a break. I think I need some time to think.

I've been throwing myself into work and the cleanup ever since last year. I think I spent all that time focused on helping and cleaning so that I wouldn't have time to think. And that was probably a good thing. But now I need to rethink my priorities.

OK, so what do I know?

I know I am drinking too much. It's not a good thing. I should never drink alone. It's damned easy to cry when you're drinking all by yourself. I cried last night. Nothing good is going to come out of sitting in a trailer, drinking and crying alone. So that should be a rule. It's too easy to become a drunk when you are depressed, so the rule is: Don't drink alone.

I'm feeling a little better already. Rule number one. Check. Never drink by myself. Too depressing. I am not going to be that depressed drunk guy. No siree.

OK, now then, what's next on the list? If I take away drinking alone, then I should probably add something good. What am I missing in my life? What makes me happy? Well, that's actually pretty easy. Sailing makes me happy. I haven't been able to do much sailing this past year with all the cleanup. I miss sailing. I need to spend some more time back on my boat. All this rebuilding has taken away my time for sitting and breathing. The best times of my life were spent on a boat in the water, sitting back and enjoying the moment. I haven't been able to enjoy a moment in a long time.

Check rule number two then. I'm going to become an active member of the Biloxi Yacht Club. It's time to reconnect with the water. Make friends again.

I have never underestimated the power of water. It's time to heal.

I drove along feeling satisfied with myself for making choices. Taking the time to think about my life and rearrange my priorities. I was not going to drink alone and I was going to reconnect with the water. That felt good.

What else do we got? Work. Let's have ourselves a chat about work. I love my job. I'm good at what I do, and I've been doing it a long time. I think I've been doing it for too long, though. I think it might be time to retire. I don't need the money anymore. Money is not a big deal. I got plenty of money.

If I don't work, then what will I do? I know the answer to that one as clear as day. I want to help others. Other people helped me when I needed it, and it's time for me to give back.

I've been a volunteer with the Shriners for a while, and I think instead of driving every day to New Orleans, I'm going to devote my time to helping others. I mean, have you ever looked at some of those kids? Those little kids with birth defects and cleft palates? God made them without their little legs? It's sad. I can help.

I must have been quite a sight when I pulled up at work that day. I don't remember a time when I walked so determinedly through any doors. Went up to my boss and told him of my plan to retire. To give back. He was sad to see me go, I know. But I was proud.

Today

Today I am remarried. I have rebuilt my life, my home, and my family. I devote my time and energy to the Shriners. I give back.

There is nothing that competes with helping others heal. We all see miracles every day. Every day we have opportunities to help others. In my mind, I see this one boy that we worked with who was born with physical disabilities. His legs were impaired enough that I see him in a wheelchair with braces on his legs. He worked with us for a while, and one day I got to see that boy come out of the backseat of a van and walk twenty feet across the parking lot to us. Miracles every day.

We are all blessed with opportunities.

CHAPTER 5

Buddies: Joseph's Story

Before Trauma: Just a Kid

EVERYTHING I KNOW ABOUT JOSEPH, I am about to tell you. Some stories, like this one, don't need an introduction.

When I think about Iraq, I think about the people I knew. A lot of different shit happened over there, but I remember the guys, you know, like Lodge. Staff Sergeant Stephen Lodge was a great guy. He was old guard. He was in a different platoon than me at first, but got changed over. We were the same age. We're both married, although he and his wife got pregnant after our first deployment. He also got promoted before I did. He was a good dude. The kind of dude the army needs. And he loved the army. We used to sit and listen to the radio together, hung out a lot.

When I think of Lodge, I think of the "penetrator." I don't know why he called our workouts the penetrator, but he loved that name and he loved working out. He was an intense guy.

During the penetrator workout for PT, we would start with a three- or four-mile run. Then we would do a combination of pull-ups and sit-ups. We would start with one pull-up and five sit-ups, and then move on to two pull-ups, ten sit-ups, on to three pull-ups and fifteen sit-ups onward, until we hit six pull-ups and thirty sit-ups. Once we hit six pull-ups, we would work our way back down the series to one pull-up and five sit-ups. After this series, we did a combination of dips, abs, forward planks, and side planks. Believe me, he got into these workout sessions.

I remember him waking up one morning saying he couldn't sleep the night before, he was so excited about the penetrator workout. Other days, he and I would go on longer runs. Runs for, like, six miles, but we would try and run them faster. I can remember us getting six miles done in forty-two minutes. He was so interested in all of that. How fast we could go, for how long. It all made him happy and excited.

It wasn't just fitness he was interested in, though. He also got into working on his home. Before our second deployment, he would go to garage sales and look for tools. Things he could use to work on his home. He liked the idea of constant improvement. He was a great army guy.

I think of people like Billy. His real name was Robert Billadeau, but we called him Billy. He was like a kid brother to me. He was an awesome kid. Harder on himself than anyone else would be.

For example, I remember early one morning at the COP [combat outpost] in Baghdad, he and I got together to load up a bunch of shit for a mission. Our mission was to ID a bunch of guys, but we had a whole bunch of shit to get together. We had four Bradleys and four Humvees going on the mission.

Turned out the kid left his SAW [squad automatic weapon] outside on the ground where we were loading stuff up. A SAW is a machine gun, and they are all identified, so when someone loses one and it's recovered, they know who lost it. An NCO found his SAW sitting out there and turned it in to the company commander. Dude standing next to me when my company commander reported it to me said, "You gotta smoke him."

I'm thinking, you know, you can't leave your weapon lying around.

I go outside to find him, and there he is right in the spot where he left his weapon and doing push-ups. You could hear him grunting. Kid was stressed. Kid did push-ups for like half an hour.

When other guys asked me if I smoked Billy, I said, "Didn't have to. He smoked himself."

I felt bad for the kid. He was engaged once, and his fiancée broke up with him by a text message. Fucking text message to break up an engagement? That shit ain't right. He still talked to that girl every once in a while, but I didn't like it when he did. I felt like I had to protect him against her.

He was just a kid. He and I had a scary night together once over there. Our camp was set up in an old abandoned schoolhouse. It was a creepy place. We pulled watch on Tower Two one night, which meant we sat in the tower from midnight to four o'clock and watched for any noise or movement. We had radios hooked up so that we could communicate with guys located on other watchtowers, or in other areas that we couldn't see from our perspective. Cameras were also hooked up to record anything that happened. Same type of cameras as on Apaches.

Most nights on watchtowers were pretty uneventful. Even if something happened, you could figure out what it was pretty quickly from all the equipment giving us vantage points. But on this night, right after we got on duty, a cell phone rang. I knew Billy had a cell phone and figured he forgot to leave it back in the barracks.

I was like, "Fuck, Billy, you bring your cell phone?"

He looked at me with these big eyes. All I could see was his eyes searching mine. They looked scared, like he was frozen. Billy had eyes that could look scared on any given day because he didn't like to disappoint people, but this night it was that frozen look of fear.

He whispered, "I don't have my cell."

I said back to him, "Dude, look again."

He patted around his uniform while I looked into the camera to start scanning for movement. I was still pretty convinced the kid had his cell phone with him and it just rang, but it was wise to look around just in case.

He said he didn't have his phone.

Fucking cell phone was ringing, and we couldn't find out where the sound was coming from. For those of you who don't know, cell phones can be wired to set off explosives. A cell phone ringing somewhere around the tower you are sitting in is not a comforting sound. Unless you like the sound of impending death.

I asked Billy what he could see and he said, "I can't see what's going on down there. Camera doesn't let me see that area. It's in a blind spot."

So I radioed to the other tower, told them we heard a cell phone ringing, and asked them what they could see. While we waited to hear back, Billy and I made some plans. For instance, we planned to jump out if we saw a grenade pop up.

The other tower said they didn't see or hear anything. So we sat and waited. That was a scary night.

I think about Oliver too. Larry Oliver was with me from the beginning when they set up our new company, which was smaller, brigade-sized instead of battalion-sized. We were one of the first assigned in the new brigade. He was eighteen years old and a new father to twins. Married his high school sweetheart. Larry could sleep through anything. He used to set up three alarms to make sure he would get up in the morning, and he would still sleep right through them. The only thing that consistently woke him up was his wife. All we had to do was mention her name and he would wake up. Amazing. He was a little guy, only about five five, but super tough.

I knew that right away by the way he went through the Special Forces training. It's a twenty-four-day selection process that is divided into two sessions. In the first week and a half it's more individual, like the Star Course, which is hard. It's designed to see how a person will react to different things in the middle of the woods, night and day. The last two-week session is the team part, which is designed to see how you work with others and how you solve problems. You can't quit this selection process, and if you do quit, you can't go back. You're done.

But the arches in Larry's feet collapsed during the process, and he was in a lot of pain. Still wouldn't quit, though. Wanted to work through it anyway. He was ordered to talk to a medic and still wouldn't quit, even though the medic told him he was physically injured. He finally had to give in, but the way he hung in there showed that he was super tough.

I never really saw him upset. He was happy-go-lucky.

On our first deployment, the first bad thing that happened, happened to him. That kinda sucked. We had swapped out guys and were going down this street. Larry was the gunner, meaning that he was on top of our vehicle scanning for action. I was down inside the vehicle and couldn't see. A vehicle started approaching from about fifty meters behind us and another vehicle pulled out and around it. Larry yelled at this other vehicle to stop and fired a warning shot. Vehicle didn't stop immediately, which engaged Larry, and he fired again and again. He started screaming down, "Go! Go! Go!"

I was thinking, what the fuck? If he just shot and killed someone, we can't leave. I couldn't see what happened, but I knew that we couldn't just leave. And a fucking horn was going off outside.

Meanwhile Larry was frantic and screaming for us to go. We looked up and assessed what was going on, and saw this vehicle with someone leaned over the steering wheel. I realized the dude must have been leaning on the horn, which was that incessant sound. Plus, you could still hear Larry freaking out. The Iraqi police were also standing there, but they weren't doing anything.

Part of me looked at them and thought, "This is your country, go figure it out," as we thought about whether we should leave or not.

We stayed and took care of the situation. The dude that was shot was like seventy-five years old and had a hearing aid. Probably couldn't hear the warning shot or the yelling, so kept approaching us anyway. He had one round in his cheek in his face, one in his right arm, and one in his side. Every time his heart beat, blood squirted out of his arm.

Larry was upset. "I killed him. I killed him."

I told him, "You're OK."

We pulled the guy out of the vehicle and handed him over to the Iraqi police so they could take him to the hospital.

Larry was shook up about the situation. Our commander talked to him and told him that he didn't do anything wrong. It wasn't intentional. He was responding to the situation at hand. The guy's family was paid. Guy was just old.

This happened about a week before he was supposed to go on leave, and he decided he didn't want to tell his wife about it until after his leave was over. He needed time to get away from the situation and didn't want to worry her. Problem was that another first sergeant told his wife, who told Larry's wife, and then Larry's wife freaked out. She got all worried that he was keeping stuff from her.

We got all over that guy for telling his wife. Can't start wife drama, which is a shit storm, because we have enough to deal with over here and they are only going to worry more if they hear about stuff like that. It's not helpful. Dude said he didn't care. Was still going to tell his wife stuff. Whatever.

It was bad, though, because that was really the first bad thing that happened to us over there and it happened to him. It was the first time he had killed anyone.

It is definitely disturbing to harm someone unintentionally. I remember one time it happened to me. We were pulling guard duty up in the towers and a vehicle approached. I yelled down, "Stop! Go away!" Asshole got out of his car and put his hands up in the air and said something to me. I was like, "No way, dude, you gotta go." He still moved forward, so I fired a warning shot. The bullet ricocheted off the rim of the tire of the car and looked like it hit the lady sitting in the passenger seat. I was like, "What the fuck?"

At that point, he made the decision to finally jump back in his car and drive away. I was left sitting there wondering, "What just happened? Did I really just shoot that woman?" It wasn't intentional and she still could have lived. I worried about that moment for a long time. I definitely wasn't trying to murder anyone. Protocol is that you tell them to stop, and fire a warning shot. I fired toward the ground and it ricocheted. That was crazy and I felt really bad about it. Talked to a bunch of people and everyone told me not to worry. That she was probably OK. I just remember the way she slumped over, though. That slump didn't look good to me. I see it pretty vividly in my mind. Looked like the life went right out of her.

It was hard to watch the way some of the Iraqi people were dealing with the situation in their country. I can't tell you how many times a situation would occur, and the Iraqis would run away while we ran toward the situation. How are you going to fix your country if you can't handle the crises of the moment? I remember during our first deployment, we saw lots of car bombs and suicide bombers. We were close to all of it but didn't get touched. We'd go and help pick up all the body parts. All Iraqis, but the Iraqi people would run away. I would think, "If you want your country back, go get it. This is it."

One time, around this Iraqi police station, a Jeep Grand Cherokee exploded. There was all this freaking and screaming. Someone shot at me, so I shot back. Killed him. I shot at another guy and he blew up.

Suicide bombers die gruesome deaths. Their heads come clean off. Legs and arms come off. This guy's head came clean off. When I walked over to look at it, the head didn't look real anymore. It looked like wax. Both of his eyes were open and he had a chipped tooth. I said to the head, "Retard. Why did you do that?" Unfortunately, I also tripped over another guy's body and felt his rib cage. Four or five years later and it is still hard to eat spareribs.

One of the worst experiences in Iraq happened with the Iraqi security forces. We were asked to come in and contain the situation, but it was a bad situation. You could tell as soon as you walked outside the building. The smell was terrible. Sunni guards had rounded up about 150 Shiite people and kept them prisoner in these two rooms. It was unclear how long they had been there or for what reason they were there. It was like a concentration camp. We carried around bars of soap and put them under our noses just to smell something normal. That's how bad the smell was.

It was dark and crowded and awful. All the guys locked up were super skinny. One guy had a cut in his ass that was diamond shaped. You could tell it was an intentional injury someone did to him to harm him. There was one bathroom in the cell and a bunch of piss bottles lying around. The piss in the bottles was an amber/red color. It was dark.

I got so angry. How could anyone treat people like this? When we asked them what they had done to be imprisoned, they said it was because they were Shiite.

We were there for the first twenty-four hours to contain the situation. We rotated all the prisoners through the stations. They were allowed to use the bathroom and clean themselves up. We brought in food and water. None of the prisoners or the guards were allowed to leave the building. One of the Iraqi army dudes tried to leave and fought with me. I was so angry at the way he had treated other human beings that I hit him back and threw him down the stairs. There were only about eight stairs. Sergeant stopped me on my way down to hit him again and told me to go outside and catch my breath. We kept the guards downstairs for the first day and were ordered to lay waste to anything that tried to come back upstairs.

A couple of days later there was a huge explosion about four blocks away from the concentration camp. Two jeeps had been packed full of C-four [a plastic explosive]. The explosion was so huge that the doors opened up where we were. An entire block was rubble. A van was thrown up in a tree. It totally destroyed the neighborhood and took a chunk out of the earth. Water mains opened, and water was shooting up in the air. What the fuck?

I found a three-year-old girl in the rubble. She was dead and I took her body to an aid station. There was a lot of crying that day.

TRAUMA: **Stuffed Pork Chops**

In our second deployment to Iraq, we had ten KIAs [killed in action]. Numbers 3,998, 3,999, and 4,000 were among them. The news of number 4,000 made headlines across the nation. The news changed my life forever. They were my buddies.

Easter Sunday that year fell on March 23, 2008. It was also my mom's birthday. It was a bad day in Iraq. We were stationed in southern Baghdad and had been getting shelled all day. We were sent out that morning to do cleaning missions. This means after you've been mortared a lot, you go out on four-hour missions to find out who had been doing the shellings.

Our investigative methods involved putting up signs that said, "If you have any information on these crimes, please call this number." That day we got one response. There was one lady who wanted to talk to us, but she got nervous when her husband came around, and she changed her mind. She decided not to talk to us.

We made a couple more stops and searched a vehicle, but nothing turned up. We told each other that we would see each other back at the command base. We had been spending a lot of time out at the FOB [forward operations base], which is a smaller base that doesn't have as much as the command base. Since we had been getting hit so hard, we weren't allowed back to the FOB. This was OK with us because we were ready to go back to the COP and its better accommodations, like stuffed pork chops.

The convoy back had three American vehicles and two Iraqi police vehicles. The lead and the trail vehicles were Bradley tanks. I was supposed to be on that lead Bradley but ended up on the trail Bradley.

When you go out on a mission, you get a trip ticket. The trip ticket will have every vehicle and all personnel on it. For this mission, Stoller and I were supposed to be on the lead Bradley, but Lodge and I talked before the return home and decided to switch. I kept Stoller with me, and we went to the trail Bradley.

The lead Bradley A1-1 (which stands for Apache First Platoon—First vehicle) held:

Driver: Private Second Class Sánchez
Gunner: Specialist Del Rio
Bradley Commander: Sergeant Oliver
Dismounts: Staff Sergeant Lodge and Private First Class Billadeau

The trail Bradley A1-4 (Apache First Platoon—Fourth vehicle) held:

Driver: Private First Class Rogers
Gunner: Sergeant Branch
Bradley Commander: First Lieutenant Cooke
Dismounts: Sergeant Braun (me) and Specialist Stoller

We switched positions because we didn't want the two highest-ranking dudes on the mission to be on the same vehicle in case something happened. If they both had gone down, I would have had to leave Stoller to handle things on the ground in order to make communications with Battalion, Company, and Air Assets.

Stuffed pork chops were on our mind during the return. Stoller and I were listening to "Ten Rounds with José Cuervo" on Stoller's iPod. Outside, the front Bradley exploded. I didn't hear the explosion. The tank was hit with a fifteen-inch EFP [explosively formed projectile] detonated with an iPod. When you are inside the pocket, you can't hear the blast. Plus, you can't see shit inside a Bradley. The song kept playing, Stoller and I tapping along. The Iraqis in the second car saw the explosion. They jumped out and started running. In the other direction. The Americans in the third car engaged. We could hear firing now. But the music still played . . .

The firing got our attention, and we jumped out of the Bradley to see what was going on. We ran forward to clear the vehicle. I saw the fire and thought we hit something and made it explode. I also saw someone running toward us on fire. It was weird because he spoke perfect English. I heard him say, "Stoller, put me out!" In the background of my mind, the song continued to play. The guy on fire spoke clear English, and I wasn't thinking about his accent. I still thought this was an Iraqi that we had hit.

Stoller said back to him, "Stop, drop, and roll! Stop, drop, and roll!"

He was naked. The clothes had burned off of him.

Most of the Iraqi police that were with us ran as soon as the firing started, but one guy stayed, and he was the guy that jumped on top of the man on fire to put him out.

Stoller looked at him and said to me, "That's Oliver."

I was like, "What?"

Why would he think the guy on fire was Larry? It was hard to tell anything about him.

Stoller said, "Look at his arm."

Larry had a tattoo on his arm. He had kids. Twins. And this guy had a tattoo on his arm.

It was Larry.

Oh, shit. That's when I looked up and saw the Bradley on fire.

We ran toward the Bradley and got hit from someone firing up in the windows. We were getting shot at and started to engage.

"Kill everything," I said, as I grabbed Stoller. In my mind, I was thinking we needed to get Larry off the street. Try and get in that building where they were shooting at us. I didn't want to see Larry lying in the street. Our radio wasn't working, the machine gun wasn't working, we couldn't get into the fucking building where they were shooting at us because they had chains on the doors and the windows were barred.

"Fuck. Need to get in there. Kill anyone in there."

We had nothing but peashooters, and we couldn't get in the building. We kept shooting and waiting for others to show up for backup. We only had two or three rounds left.

Suddenly the Bradley lunged forward, leaving Stoller and me without cover. So we ran over and hid behind this Iraqi car. One of the translators stayed with us. His name was James, and he was one of the few Iraqis that would hang in there when shit started to happen. Stoller and I kept shooting to hold them off.

I was thinking, "My wife is going to be so pissed off when she hears about this. I hope I die before Stoller. I don't want to watch him die." I looked over at him and he was scanning for a moving target. I figured that I might as well kill as much as I could before I went down.

Larry was moaning in the background. I could hear him but was not looking at him. He kept saying, "Oh my God, I'm going to die." I said, "No you're not, bro. We got you."

Another target moved and I heard James scream, "Fuck you" at him in English. It's funny to think of him saying that now.

I don't know how much I killed, but we shot out all of the windows in the building. And the rest of the platoon showed up. The squad started the process of cleaning up.

Stoller looked at me and said, "I thought we were going to get killed."

I said, "I did too. I was hoping to go before you. I didn't want to watch you die."

He looked at me and said, "That is exactly what I was thinking. I wanted to go before you."

We had a helicopter coming in. Colonels, the commander, and the platoon all came out.

Cross focused on cleaning out the vehicle that got hit. He burned his hands because the vehicle was so hot. He saw Lodge and Billy were gone, but they were not burned. They were stuck in the hatch.

We were still focusing on getting Larry out of there. A tank came down and started shooting over his head. King had a stretcher and Larry was put on it, but the stretcher was too long for the back of the Bradley, so I sat in there with him to hold him. Put his head on my lap. When the door closed, I banged it back to tell them to go. Move out. I was screaming to get going.

I realized that I couldn't get shot in the back of the Bradley and felt grateful for a second, and then the selfishness of that thought hit me.

Larry's forehead was about the only part of him that looked good. His shoulder was melted to his skin and he was naked. The clothes melted right off of him. His foot was melted into his boot.

We were having a hard time getting a vein for an IV. He was losing time.

At that point outside, Cross was trying to get Billy out of the vehicle, but it was too hot. Rounds started exploding around him. He was told to get the fuck out of there.

We were told the status was five minutes, but it felt like hours until we slowed down. When the Bradley slowed, Larry rolled off of me a little bit and his skin came off on my vest. I didn't want to hurt him any more than he was already hurt.

He said, "Tell my wife and kids I love them."

I said, "No, man, you're good."

He coughed and red foam came out of his mouth. He was getting worse. I took off his helmet.

We still didn't know anything about the other guys. We were thinking that maybe they got out. Maybe it was just Larry that got hurt.

The crew was there to take Larry when we stopped and they wheeled him away. They asked us about the four other guys, and we said that we didn't know where they were.

Me, Stoller, and Rogers cleared our weapons to go in with Larry. As we parked, someone said, "You can't park your Bradley here."

I screamed, "Hey, retard, I'm in no mood. I'm going to fuck you up. I'm going to put it right here. I don't give a fuck."

I walked off.

Inside we hugged each other and drank some water.

What the hell? It's hard to even register what we had just been through. What we were going through at that minute. Bringing Larry in injured like that, going through that firefight, thinking that we weren't going to make it. I couldn't believe it all had just happened.

We sat there for a while not really talking. About ten minutes later, Conley, our commander, walked up and gave us hugs. I didn't know what to say. He said, "You all right?" I asked about the rest of the guys. Sergeant Washington walked in then and said, "I thought you were dead." I said, "You better not tell my wife that."

I still didn't know what had happened. The trip ticket had the assignments of all the vehicles and personnel on the mission. One Bradley from our trip did not return.

Sergeant Washington thought I was dead because I was assigned to the lead Bradley. But instead Lodge and I decided to make a switch to balance leadership.

It was like a kick in the gut when I found out they were all dead. We sat there waiting for news of Larry and didn't leave until two in the morning. The majority of the company came out. We sat around, waiting. Our platoon leader came and everyone hugged. The colonel came, and true to his politician self he said that we were not going to retaliate. I hate that guy.

That was a long night. There are no good words to explain what it feels like to hear that your buddies were just brutally murdered while you wait to hear news of another one fighting for his life. It's like time is completely different. Time usually goes by pretty quickly, but when you are waiting to hear about life or death, time slows. It becomes tangible in some way. You could touch the emotions coming out of all of us. Time is fuzzy, though, too. I remember us all sitting there together, but you couldn't really tell how much time had passed. Could've been five minutes or five hours. It's a terrible feeling to sit and wait for news.

Even your thoughts become fuzzy, but also more clear. Maybe because the time you spend waiting feels like an eternity, so you have more time to sit and think about what you are thinking about. You can't distract yourself with other thoughts. You can't just get up and take care of anything. You sit there, waiting, worrying, feeling. It sucks.

I wanted Larry to make it. We all wanted Larry to make it. Thoughts of the guys who didn't make it were bouncing around my head. I couldn't focus on any one thought for too long because I had all these images of these guys bouncing around. And someone would say something to make me think about other images. It was really hard to concentrate. And really hard to focus. I wanted revenge.

I am glad we were there together. It was a lot easier to have everyone there together. We all felt the same thing.

They finally came and told us that Larry was being shipped off to Germany. We got to see him go by on a gurney. He was in a plastic bag. Ninety-two percent of his body was burned.

When a soldier dies, the army enforces a communication blackout. We are not to have contact with anyone back home. This is so they have time to contact the family members of the deceased. It is out of respect so the family doesn't hear about their loved one some other way. I understand, because I wouldn't want my wife to find out something like that about me off the cuff. I would want her to hear the details. The problem with communication blackouts is that everyone back home knows something happened. And then they worry. They want to know it wasn't their person killed. They might see some news story that U.S. soldiers were involved in a firefight and that four were killed. And they might hear where the firefight happened and know that their person is right there. Their person could have been involved. Their person could have been killed. So they sit and worry about that knock on the door. That's what the army does. They send people out to your home to tell the news in person. You don't want your family to worry that it is you when you are OK. So I decided to send an e-mail to my wife that night that read:

I'm OK. I'm alive. I need you to be strong. Tell my parents I'm OK. Take care of the other wives and families.

That was my way of letting her know that I was OK, but that she was going to be needed.

I was angry at Arab Muslims. I hated them. I knew it was stupid, but my buddies were being murdered in this cowardly way. And it was only March, which means I was still going to be there for a long time. No time to think about it right then because I needed to take care of my other soldiers. I thought I should try and keep my mood light for the guys.

But I was feeling anything but light.

Our squad was down from nine to four. We had some logistics to figure out. First thing we had to do was get the guys' stuff ready to be shipped back to their families. Get stuff off their computers. Pack up all their stuff.

It was really strange to have their areas cleaned up and gone. Seemed like at any moment one of them might come around the corner and show up. Hard to appreciate the fact that I would never see them pop through a door again, hear them around a corner, talk to them about what happened.

That was maybe the hardest part. I couldn't talk to them about what happened. Couldn't tell them what I saw and did. Couldn't ask them how it felt. Couldn't tell them what happened next. Couldn't even say good-bye.

Everything was different right away. It felt like everyone was looking at Stoller and me differently. We'd been involved in the firefight on a different level than the rest of the guys.

Everything had changed.

SYMPTOMS: **The Stand-In**

Some people have really cool jobs—the types of jobs that make you wonder how they even got them. For example, Jerry Remy is a color commentator for the Boston Red Sox. He played for the Red Sox in the late 1970s and has been the team's announcer for many years. You imagine conversations took place that allowed him to become the guy who attends and describes details of every game to the viewing and listening audience.

People have been listening to this guy's voice for years. It must be the case that many people hear Jerry Remy's voice and feel like he is talking directly to them, telling them the details of each game their favorite team plays. He must feel like a member of people's families. Jerry has been present for many Fourth of July parties, birthday celebrations, Memorial Day and Labor Day festivities—parties for people he has never even met.

Other people do not have such cool jobs. You've all seen that person standing by the side of the road wearing some type of sandwich board advertisement, or worse, some cartoonish outfit, to market a service or business. Perhaps that individual enjoys what he does. At some level, it might be fun to stand outside dressed like a wiener to draw customers to Hot Dog Heaven.

The person who chose to stand on the street dressed like a hot dog put himself in a position to do that job. Perhaps he sought out that experience, or somehow he applied for a position where he knew wearing the costume might be one of the job requirements. In any event, people choose what they do.

The same is true for people who join the military. Perhaps they have always wanted to be soldiers. Perhaps they wanted to become physicians, but the only way they could afford to fund their schooling was to join the service. Perhaps they have had ancestors and family members in the military, and the expectation was that they would join as well. Perhaps they joined the National Guard and intended to help their countrymen and -women during times of national distress. Whatever the case, all individuals in the military chose to join the military. They volunteered.

After joining the military, each individual then undergoes extensive basic training. During times of war, extensive training is administered to prepare servicemen and -women for combat. They are trained to engage in battle, fire weapons, evade fire, band together, obey orders, and think in the moment. To be battle ready, service members must be physically fit, and physical training is an important component of battle readiness.

Mental preparation is also critical. Courses and instruction on all aspects of mental preparedness are administered prior to deployment. Service members learn strategies and weaponry and about warfare. Another important component of mental readiness involves uniformity. Uniforms are standard issue and worn daily. Basic operations such as roll call and cleaning your quarters are fixed and mandatory. There are definitive rules and regulations.

Emotional training also takes place. Each serviceman and -woman attends courses on battle preparedness, including training on symptoms associated with trauma. They learn about trauma and post-traumatic stress disorder—what to look for in themselves, what to look for in others, and what to do if these symptoms occur.

All servicemen and -women must have wills on file before their deployment to war. Wills are prepared after conversations take place with family members and military personnel. Servicemen and -women prepare for death.

Not only are they mentally prepared for battle and death, but they are also prepared and trained for their return home. They learn that they must revert, emotionally and mentally, to a civilian mind-set.

For example, in combat, driving fast and changing lanes unpredictably may save your life. At home, this same style of driving would likely get you a ticket. In combat, survival may depend on your ability to discipline subordinates and obey orders. At home, this same rigidity will likely cause conflict with family members and friends.

Servicemen and -women prepare for combat. Yet all these preparations may still be inadequate for the reality of war. The real training happens on the battlefield.

Reexperiencing

I had a nightmare two nights ago. It's one that I have often. In the dream, my squad is in Baghdad. On patrol. It is dark and hot out, and suicide bombers keep coming. Firing. Every time they fire, an explosion happens about two feet away from me. The explosions are basically right on top of me. I feel the heat. I know I am supposed to be dead, but every time the explosion happens, I keep on walking. I am OK. But anyone next to me is dead. I can't stop anyone from dying and I can't make myself die. Nothing I do matters. It doesn't matter if I hold on to someone or if I try and cover that person up; they die, and I walk away unscathed.

My nightmares were so horrible at first. I had one that actually made me piss my bed. I wasn't eating, wasn't sleeping. Just walking around in a haze. They made me talk to a counselor over there, who prescribed Ambien for sleep, and an antidepressant.

I thought, "Are you fucking kidding me?" I lost faith in the help of mental health if all they were going to do was give me medicine. What the fuck kind of help is that? I threw all the medicine away.

Stoller and I talked often about that night. What we would've done differently. If we had used the bazooka? Nothing would've mattered, though. They would have died anyway.

Avoidance

It is hard to feel motivated about anything. I just don't care anymore. I've gotten what I want out of the military. They've taken more from me than I took from them. Take me out of the fight. If they put me in Iraq or Afghanistan today, I would do my job, but I don't care anymore. I used to care. But I don't anymore.

The fight went out of me right away after those guys died. I didn't sleep or eat much for a couple of weeks after. We were still getting hit at the time, and I didn't know how we were going to fight them off. My platoon was hit too bad. We needed replacements.

Larry had left Germany and was settled in a hospital in Texas getting treatments for his burns. On June tenth, we found out he wasn't doing good. At nine fifteen, we got a warning about his status. At eleven thirty, we found out he was gone. It was my one ray of hope: that I was going to get to see him when I was on leave. Cross got to see him when he was on leave, but it was too late for me.

My heart sank when I heard the news. I had the most empty feeling. What the fuck are we doing this for? Can't we catch a break? I'm done. I just don't care anymore.

My leave was at the end of August, and by July I didn't care at all. If someone asked me to do something, I would say, "Fuck you."

I was so stressed out. I couldn't deal with any of it anymore. It was bad enough that my first sergeant pulled me aside. He said to me, "Listen, you're not in trouble or anything, but you have to pull it together."

I said, "I don't care anymore. I can't deal with it. We're a nine-man squad, and we're down to four. What the fuck? We're still getting mortared constantly and nothing has changed." He asked if I needed a break. I said yes.

That made everything worse, though. There are only so many movies you can watch. I sat in a tent for seven straight days and watched movies. I learned that there is such a thing as too much time on your hands. It was shitty.

After leave, our squad was so decimated that strings were pulled so that we didn't have to go on missions anymore. No more house searches. We couldn't do anything anymore. We drove around and talked to people.

We also built T-walls. T-walls were intended to be security devices. They are twelve-foot-high walls made of cement. They are set up to help absorb the blast from an explosion. They are set up all over Iraq now and used for all sorts of purposes. Many of them are even painted.

I was so bored, though. I would ask to play on the crane used to lift the concrete piece for the T-wall. I wasn't supposed to be on the crane, but I didn't care. We were so bored, we did things like practice shooting out lights.

You would think I had plenty of time to work out, or do something useful. I did have the time. But I didn't care anymore. Plus, I didn't have my partner for PT. He was dead. Everyone I worked out with was dead. And I couldn't do the penetrator workout without him.

Fuck this, I quit. I'm doing my time until I get out.

Hyperarousal

Their deaths got a lot of press. Numbers 3,998, 3,999, and 4,000 killed in the war in Operation Iraqi Freedom. It was the big time in terms of news. At the funeral there were a lot of VIPs because number 4,000 was killed. Fuck them. They said stuff and acted all concerned, but they didn't know those guys. They didn't know them.

I feel guilty that I made it and they didn't. There was nothing glorious about the way that they died. It was just brutal. And I never want to forget them. Forgetting them would be dishonoring their memory or something. I don't want to do that. Seemed to me that the only thing I could do was make sure that the guys' families were OK. I tried to contact everyone's family as soon as I could after the explosion.

Del Rio's wife was gone and I couldn't get ahold of her. I tried to find her to talk to her but couldn't.

Sánchez's family was hard to find at first, but I finally managed to talk with them. He had left a bunch of stuff at our house before the deployment, and my wife was able to give his family his stuff. She even went out to dinner with his mom, sister, and uncle, which I thought was awesome. It was hard because it was upsetting, but she and I both felt like it was an important thing to do. I think they appreciated it.

I called Lodge's wife and she wanted to know everything that had happened. I told her about that night. She was not doing well, and we tried to be there for her. She had the baby to take care of, and she was really upset. Gruesome because it was hard to get him out of the Bradley after the explosion because of the heat, so he came back in pieces. His leg was sent home. She wanted to see it, but I told her not to. I still talk to her every couple of months.

Larry Oliver's wife got to spend time with him before he died. She had the time to see him, touch him, and say good-bye. He was on a lot of pain medicines for the burns, so he wasn't always coherent. But they got to say good-bye. Being able to say good-bye makes a big difference. I still talk to her.

I talk often to Billy's family. He had a little brother who played baseball in college until he blew out his shoulder. He was an awesome kid. Awesome family.

I feel like I need to be there for all of these people. Doing anything else would be dishonorable. And if you feel differently, go fuck yourself. I don't care what you think.

Survivor's guilt was first recognized among survivors of the Holocaust. It is not an unusual response to surviving combat or a natural disaster when others did not survive. Survivor's guilt is a form of anxiety associated with posttraumatic stress disorder. Treatment for survivor's guilt often involves treatments associated both with the trauma and with the grief associated with the trauma. Individuals experiencing survivor's guilt work toward closure as part of their healing.

Closure is a necessary component of many relationships and events we endure throughout our lives, but is most commonly associated with grief surrounding death.

Closure in this case was complicated by the fact that closure, or saying good-bye, felt dishonorable. Joseph wants these men remembered. By dedicating his time to telling his story, he was able to pay tribute to his friends and the brutal way they were murdered without dishonoring their memory. He told the story the way he experienced it.

It is my hope that in sharing his story, Joseph experienced some closure. Our purpose in telling his story was solely to pay tribute, and we never discussed the idea that he might benefit or be harmed by talking about his experiences. Yet in describing his fellow soldiers and what they went through together, he may have created an opportunity to begin to forgive himself for surviving. He may begin to feel free to make the next move toward his own life and freedom.

Joseph was agitated that their memorials received attention solely due to the number. Number 4,000 dead in Iraq. His belief was that they should be honored because they were honorable servicemen, not because of a number.

Joseph also expressed irritation over the idea of moving forward away from this incident. Some of the wives began dating over time, and although he was able to understand the need for creating a stable family environment for the children involved, he was also concerned. He did not articulate the exact nature of this concern, although it seemed apparent that he did not want those men forgotten. May all of us have friends like Joseph.

Joseph has an amazing life ahead. When we first began working together to tell this story, I asked him to start at the beginning and to tell me something about himself. He instead began talking about the night of the firefight. It was the story that he wanted to tell and in some ways was both the beginning and the end for him. It should be noted that he knew other men and friends killed in action in Iraq, but this experience was the one that changed him. This was the one that mattered. This was the one that birthed a new awareness of life and friendship and meaning.

The meaning of the war changed for Joseph after that night, and with it went his energy. He has a solid support system, including a loving and supportive wife and family. Although his life is in transition now due to this event, I believe Joseph will emerge stronger.

RECOVERY: **Remembrance**

I used to not understand what difference it made if you could keep your room clean. Being in the army, though, teaches you why it matters. If you can't follow simple instructions like cleaning up your room, then how would it be possible for you to sit in a guard tower for four straight hours and keep watch to make sure everyone stays safe? Being able to follow instructions and stay on task matters.

It's not easy to be a leader. Some people are natural-born leaders. In the military, the natural-born leaders tend to move on to other careers. The bad soldiers tend to stay put. They figure there is nothing else they can really do. And you can tell the difference between a good soldier and a bad soldier right away.

I want a career that is challenging. I wanted to go into the army, and I wanted to go to war. I've been to war twice, and I can tell you that the first time you are getting shot at is enough. I remember the first time I was shot at. It didn't even register at first that real bullets were coming at me. I got behind cover and started to engage, and that's when the thought first hit me. I thought, "What are you trying to kill me for? Fuck you! I didn't do anything to you!" The first time I was fired at was enough. You can keep that shit.

I'm in the infantry and guys in the infantry can be treated pretty shitty. I want to look forward to work. It can come down to respect and honor. I don't care what people think of me. I want people to get something done. My leadership style isn't to scream or yell. If someone does something wrong, then he has to be jacked up. Got to smoke him to make him get it. Bring the pain. But the majority of my soldiers are good dudes. You can just talk to them and they will get it. I never had an issue with disrespect. I would rather teach. My message isn't that I am better than you. My message is that I will lead with you. Lead from the front. It's not "do as I say" but "do as I do."

But every once in a while, you have to smoke someone. It's corrective training. You know, like giving them push-ups. For example, formation happens at six o'clock. At five thirty, I check the barracks and make sure that they didn't go out the night before and are still acting like retards. If someone is not acting like he is going to be ready for formation, I might say something like, "Dude, get ready." If he is still not ready at six fifteen, I might say, "Hey, I checked, what happened?" If that person mouths off or rolls his eyes at me, especially if he does it in front of a superior or peers and makes me look bad, I gotta smoke him. It's important that everyone does his job.

One of my pet peeves is when a guy doesn't do his job. Part of your job in the military is to not use drugs. We have drug tests. So if someone fails a drug test, it's like, "You're an idiot." That person is not worth it.

Worse if someone goes AWOL. It's like a peripheral "Fuck you." It's like that person is saying that his life is more important than yours. I'm like, "Are you retarded? We are at war." All of our lives are important. And interconnected. That's what some people just don't seem to get.

I want to be remembered. A part of my childhood died recently. The Seattle Mariners announcer, Dave Niehaus, died at the age of seventy-five. It makes me teary-eyed to talk about it. I feel like I lost my grandpa. I've been listening to him broadcast Mariner baseball games since I was a little kid.

I heard about his death driving over to my dad's house. The radio announcer said it so nonchalantly that I couldn't believe it really happened. Apparently he had a heart attack on his back deck. He was on his back deck about to eat barbecued ribs for dinner. Had a heart attack and died instead.

Niehaus was old school. He wasn't afraid to speak his mind. I would love to go to school and study broadcasting. I went on one website recently and listened to a broadcaster who was so bad at it that I wanted to punch my computer. With Niehaus, blind people could see the game through his announcing.

I sat and listened to sports talk radio the day he died. They had an all-day tribute to him. You know, Niehaus was real. I want to be real like that.

Don't get me wrong, I'm proud of what I did in Iraq. But I've done my part and I'm ready to move on. I don't want to worry my wife anymore. I don't want the responsibility of worrying about my guys or the guys under me getting killed.

Basically, I decided I can't live the life I'm living anymore. I've gained twenty pounds. I have no motivation, no drive. I just don't care. I am ready to get out of the military. I don't feel like I can get any more out of it. I got leadership, rank, and confidence out of my time in. I was successful and I earned respect.

I was the leader I wanted to be. I will bust my ass with my men. I will even burn crap with the guys. We did it together. Setting down track is actually the worst job ever. Worse than burning crap. I did it with them. But now, when I drive to work in the morning, I hope for a car accident so I can't make it in. I hate doing my job in the army now.

I am going to make a change. After my time is done in the service, I'm going into broadcasting. I want to do more. The other thing that has to change is the way I feel. I am tired of feeling shitty about the whole situation. I can't continue feeling this bad. The weekend has been crazy, we had five guys get DUIs this weekend, and one guy had a fluke accident and shot himself in the foot. It's just time to make a change.

I am alive because I want to live. I want to be happy living. I want my children and my wife to be happy.

I felt really uneasy going to my squad leader for help, but it was time. I told him that I was still really upset about what happened in

Iraq. He said it was OK. It wasn't my fault. He also said that I needed to go and talk to someone. I shouldn't still be upset.

So I went down to mental health and got scheduled for treatment for PTSD, and had two nightmare-resolution classes.

Nightmare-resolution classes are interesting. You change your dreams. One class is spent with everyone talking about his nightmares, and the next one is figuring out how to have a new outcome. My nightmares always focus on how everyone around me dies. I survive, and I can't protect them from dying. No matter what I do.

The first nightmare-resolution class had about six guys in it. We went around and each of us talked about our nightmares. I was the only guy that showed for the second nightmare class. But that's OK, because I got to work through a new outcome for my dreams. Instead of working so hard to save the guys from death, now I'm trying to say good-bye. It is important to say good-bye.

I thought going for treatment for PTSD would be hard, but it was actually a relief to be officially diagnosed. I've done my part. I'm ready to move on.

I was asked to come down to an elementary school and talk to the kids during an assembly for Veterans Day. I thought it sounded like a cool thing to do until I actually got in front of the kids. Standing in front of the kids, I asked if any of them had any questions for me. And it was precisely at that moment that I realized there are certain questions you should never ask a veteran. My guess was the kids at this school assembly wouldn't know that, though.

It ended up being cool. No one asked me the wrong kind of question. One kid asked me if I was afraid over there. I answered, "All the time." Another asked me what made me most afraid. I answered that one dishonestly. I said, "That I wouldn't see my family again. I missed my family when I was over there."

Technically, that is an honest answer. I did worry about not seeing my family again, but it wasn't what made me most afraid. I couldn't tell the kids what made me most afraid. Sometimes, it's harder to be the one that lives.

And for those of you who might not know the two questions to never ask veterans, they are:

1. Did you kill anyone?
2. Do you think we should be over there?

What I think about being at war doesn't matter to anyone. What I believe is that my guys died over there for a reason. It would be impossible for me to believe that my guys died over there for no reason at all. I couldn't accept that. I still feel guilty that I made it and they didn't. I will always feel guilty. But it is time to move on.

As they say in the army when a great man has lost his life:

Oft in the feast, and in the fight, their voices
Have mingled with our own,
Fill high the cup, but when the soul rejoices,
Forget not who are gone.

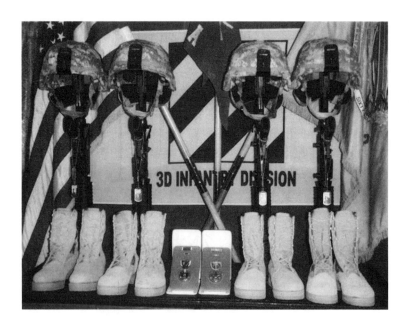

Here is a little tribute to the guys. I will take a couple of shots for them with José Cuervo. I will fill ten shot glasses.

> Round one for Del Rio:
> You were with the squad for a week and a half
> before you were killed.
> I didn't know you very well.
> It's brutal the way that you died.
> I love you, man.

And I will turn that shot glass over.

> Round two for Sánchez:
> You were driving the Bradley.
> We got on you for sending your money to your mom
> to help her with her restaurant
> but it was cool what you did.
> I love you, man.

I turn that shot glass over.

> Round three for Lodge:
> Hard to work out without you.
> You brought the energy and the fun.
> Your son lives on
> I'll make sure he is doing OK.
> I love you, man.

I turn that shot glass over.

> Round four for Billy:
> Never had to be so hard on yourself.
> You were a great kid.
> I love you, man.

I turn that shot glass over.

> Round five or six for Larry:
> We got you.
> You're OK.
> I love you, man.

> For you, man, I turn the glasses over.

Epilogue

WHEN I THINK OF CHRISTMAS, I think about presents. I love presents. I love sitting in my room and touching each one before putting them away. I love that quiet, private moment running my fingers over each new possession. That new sweater I wanted but didn't dare ask for, and how great it will be to wear with my favorite jeans. I'll wear it the very next day. My most treasured present will be placed right on top of the dresser, where I am sure to pass it by and each time experience anew the pleasure of getting it.

Perhaps I sound greedy associating Christmas with stuff. But the truth is, I love the stuff. I love to buy presents for friends and family. I love to slowly and carefully wrap and label each one. I love to pile up the wrapped treasures.

As a child, I loved the stocking. Presents in the stocking were, to me, enormously pleasing. My mother usually painstakingly wrapped each stocking stuffer as though it contained a new and wonderful surprise. I wanted to believe, so each time I unwrapped a toothbrush or pack of gum, my heart would contract with delight. Literally. I loved the idea that each gift in the stocking was both a surprise and practical. I could always use a new toothbrush, and what child doesn't like gum?

Occasionally one would find random treasures in the stocking.

A necklace, maybe, or a bracelet. Jewelry for a princess. For just that moment, I could pretend.

My mother hid all her Christmas presents on the floor of her closet, and I snooped at will. Boxes and bags thrown on top of smelly shoes and under long dresses so I had to sit on my knees and roam with my hands through the dark closet to pull out random offerings. By the time I was seven, so experienced was I in the art of sneaking that my mother enlisted me to become her elf. Realistically, this means that she gave me the task of wrapping all gifts and placing each under the tree Christmas Eve. I was elf, Santa, and slave all wrapped up in one glorious picture. And I loved it.

This year, my experience of Christmas was altered. My vision of Christmas is distorted, as though I'm looking through a crystal glass. All the pieces of Christmas still appear, but the emotion surrounding each perspective has been altered.

I've spent the last seven years working with soldiers returning from the wars in Iraq and Afghanistan. And during this year of writing these stories, my work with soldiers changed Christmas.

Sure, some soldiers are doing well and some are not. In my field, you get used to working with individuals who have disturbing stories. You learn to separate the experience of sitting with their emotions from your "self." You can sit with them while they process their emotions, and even feel their emotions with them, but feeling their emotions doesn't change you. You still go home and live your life. So it doesn't matter how many people come in to talk about why they are struggling to feel happy, or why they can't let go of some type of emotional pain, or why they would prefer to numb negative emotions through the use of substances or work or exercise or starvation or sex. You leave work that day still being you.

Until one year, this year, these soldiers changed me. They changed my entire perspective on Christmas.

I can't even explain how it happened. A number of factors may have come into play. I live in a community full of extraordinarily generous people, and it is possible that their generosity broke me down over time. It is possible that witnessing soldier and family reunions broke me down over time. It is possible that repeated conversations with veterans struggling to find work in our squeezed economy broke me over time—hearing about families that would not have Christmas.

It used to be that I could not understand things like a family deciding their Christmas gift would be making arrangements to give a goat to a needy family in Africa. Sure, that's nice. Give a goat. But give the goat and the new sweater, right? I didn't understand this form of giving.

But this year, instead of feeling warm in the idea of a new sweater, I began to feel uncomfortable. So I drummed up some energy, and my friends and I organized a Christmas drive. We wanted to give back to some of the families that were struggling because of their time at war.

I didn't change completely, you understand. I still planned to send my family their favorite gifts. I took extreme pleasure picking out a small sandbox toy for my young son. It had miniature shovels and rocks and rakes and construction vehicles that he could manipulate, all while feeling the texture of real sand on his hands. (I knew he would love feeling the sand on his hands as much as I would dislike pulling out the vacuum cleaner after each episode.)

Yes, I still took pleasure in that type of giving. But this year, for the first time, I felt discomfort in getting. Small pleasures should be enjoyed by all. Or else we all suffer. I finally got it. I finally got the goat.

I actually do know what changed me. These stories changed me. I was prepared to hear the details of each story and put together the words for others to read. I was prepared to delve inside each experience emotionally. I was excited to be able to walk around pretending to view the world from each person's perspective in order to

About the Author

TRACY STECKER, PH.D., is a psychologist at the Dartmouth Psychiatric Research Center. Her focus is on treating veterans of the Iraq and Afghanistan wars returning with PTSD or substance abuse issues, or both. Stecker's work with returning service members has been funded by the National Institute of Mental Health and the National Institute on Alcohol Abuse and Alcoholism. She developed and published a protocol titled *Using a Brief Intervention to Motivate Clients to Get Help* in collaboration with Hazelden Foundation.

Hazelden, a national nonprofit organization founded in 1949, helps people reclaim their lives from the disease of addiction. Built on decades of knowledge and experience, Hazelden offers a comprehensive approach to addiction that addresses the full range of patient, family, and professional needs, including treatment and continuing care for youth and adults, research, higher learning, public education and advocacy, and publishing.

A life of recovery is lived "one day at a time." Hazelden publications, both educational and inspirational, support and strengthen lifelong recovery. In 1954, Hazelden published *Twenty-Four Hours a Day,* the first daily meditation book for recovering alcoholics, and Hazelden continues to publish works to inspire and guide individuals in treatment and recovery, and their loved ones. Professionals who work to prevent and treat addiction also turn to Hazelden for evidence-based curricula, informational materials, and videos for use in schools, treatment programs, and correctional programs.

Through published works, Hazelden extends the reach of hope, encouragement, help, and support to individuals, families, and communities affected by addiction and related issues.

For questions about Hazelden publications, please call
800-328-9000
or visit us online at hazelden.org/bookstore.

For additional information on these stories,
*please visit **Facebook at 5 Survivors.***